ReVision

A JOURNAL OF CONSCIOUSNESS AND TRANSFORMATION

CONTENTS

The Heart of Education
Cristina Perea Kaplan, Editor

1 On the Heart of Education: An Introduction
   Cristina Perea Kaplan

11 Learning to Belong to the Multicultural Chorus
   Greg Sarris and Cristina Perea Kaplan

21 The Shamanic Heart of Education
   Stanley Krippner

23 The Heart of Education: "The Student as a Spiritual Being"
   Jean Millay

30 Restorative Practices: Healing Hurts, Remediating Wrongdoing as an Alternative to Traditional School Discipline
   Kerri Berkowitz and Cristina Perea Kaplan

35 Working with Young People in Nature: We Plant the Seeds & See What Comes
   Lucy Lewis and Juan Antonio Santisteban

40 Texts by Youth: Poems on Identity
   7th grade Students of Lawrence Cook Middle School

42 Writing the Stories to Right the World
   Jan Ogren

51 Poetry: Between Worlds
   R.L. Boyer

Book Review

53 Attachment-Based Teaching: Creating a Tribal Classroom, by Louis Cozolino
   Review by **Cristina Perea Kaplan**

Cover art by Lily A. Kaplan, age 10

Spring 2020 • Volume 33 • Number 2

What Is ReVision?

Revisioning, as the name ReVision hints, has been central to the publication's forty year historical trajectory. As our understanding of the leading edge of transformative and consciousness-changing thinking has developed, so has the focus of our mission.

From its origins in humanistic and transpersonal psychologies, ReVision has shifted toward a framework of transdisciplinary, decolonial, and indigenous paradigms. From its origins as an academic journal it has shifted toward a publication which includes art, poetry, story, and articles that translate topics for a broader audience.

With a commitment to the future of humanity and all our relations, ReVision is dedicated to the exploration of issues that assert and value the transmotional and interconnected sovereignty of people before any institutions. Sovereignty and self-determination as foundations of peace require our human imagination as part of a sustainable world of stories and cultural practices in a particular place or ecology.

ReVision welcomes submissions from a wide range of disciplines using a broad spectrum of formats to deepen the process of inquiry, dialogue, and engaged participatory knowing and conversation.

Photo by Kaplan

Volume 33, No. 2 (ISBN 978-1-7362314-0-1)

ReVision (ISSN 0275-6935) is published by
The Study of Shamanism, Healing, and Transformation.

Copyright © 2020 ReVision Publishing.
Copyright retained by author when noted. The views expressed are not necessarily those of ReVision or its editors.

ReVision provides opportunities for publishing divergent opinions, ideas, or judgments.

Manuscript Submissions

We welcome manuscript submissions.
Manuscript guidelines can be found on our webpage:
http://revisionpublishing.org.

POSTMASTER: Send address changes to
ReVision Publishing,
P.O. Box 1855,
Sebastopol, CA 95473.

Subscriptions

For subscriptions mail a check to above address or go to
www.revisionpublishing.org.

Individual Subscriptions

Subscription for one year: $36 online only,
$36 print only (international $72),
$48 print and on-line (international $84).

Subscription for two years: $60 online only,
$60 print only (international $96),
$79 print and online (international $115).

Subscription for three years: $72 online only,
$72 print only (international $108),
$96 print and online (international $132).

Institutional Subscriptions

$98 online only (international $134),
$134 print and online (international $191).

Please allow six weeks for delivery of first issue.

Editorial Board

Editor
Jürgen Werner Kremer, PhD
Santa Rosa Junior College, Santa Rosa, CA

Associate Editor
Karen Jaenke, PhD
John F. Kennedy University, Pleasant Hill, CA

Managing Editor
Cristina Perea Kaplan, MA

Editorial and Production Management Team

Denita M. Benyshek
Art Editor

Cristina Kaplan
Book Review Editor

Gary Newman
Book Designer/Production Specialist

Samuel A. Malkemus
Book Review Editor

Consulting Editors

John Adams, PhD
Saybrook University, San Francisco, CA

Matthew C. Bronson, PhD
O'Reilly Scool of Technology, UC Davis, Davis, CA

Allan Combs, PhD
California Institute of Integral Studies, San Francisco, CA

Apela Colorado
Worldwide Indigenous Science Network

Jorge Ferrer, PhD
California Institute of Integral Studies, San Francisco, CA

Mary Gomes, PhD
Sonoma State University, Rohnert Park, CA

Stanislav Grof, MD
California Institute of Integral Studies, San Francisco, CA

Stanley Krippner, PhD
Saybrook University, San Francisco, CA

Joan Marler, MA
California Institute of Integral Studies, San Francisco, CA

Alfonso Montuori, PhD
California Institute of Integral Studies, San Francisco, CA

Glenn Aparicio Parry
Circle for Original Thinking, Albuquerque, NM

Joseph Prabhu, PhD
California State University Los Angeles, CA

Donald Rothberg, PhD
Spirit Rock Meditation Center, Woodacre, CA

Meredith Sabini
The Dream Institute of Northern California, Berkeley, CA

Elenita Strobel, Ed.D
Sonoma State University, Rohnert Park, CA

ReVision Abstracts
Vol. 33 No. 2 • Spring 2020

Berkowitz, K., and Perea Kaplan, C. Restorative Practices: Healing Hurts, Remediating Wrongdoing as an Alternative to Traditional School Discipline. *ReVision*, *33*(2), 13-23. doi:10.4298/REVN.32.4.13-23

Kerri Berkowitz and Cristina Perea Kaplan explore the use of Restorative Justice Practices, or RJP, which are based on indigenous practices of repairing harm, alternatives to punitive consequences for misdeeds in the public school setting. Together they examine the positive implications of creating school-wide values, fostering trusting relationships, and using affective language to express the emotions behind behaviors and conflicts. Kerri also recounts her experience as a white South African who immigrated to the U.S., but who continued to follow the progress of Nelson Mandela's Truth and Reconciliation Commission. She offers insight from Desmond Tutu on the RJP process.

Kaplan, C.P. On the Heart of Education: An Introduction. *ReVision*, *33*(2), 13-23. doi:10.4298/REVN.32.4.13-23

Cristina Perea Kaplan explores the need to transform public K-12 education from a standards-based, business-oriented enterprise to a more balanced and psychologically focused one. She discusses holistic, humanistic, and earth grounded philosophies of education using the metaphor of the heart. Archetypal, cultural, and social-emotional competencies are explored as well as CG Jung's concept of shadow. Issues of freedom, choice, control, and strategies to empower students and teachers, such as Restorative Justice Practices are also examined. Outdoor education and a focus on nature are emphasized as the survival of humanity hangs in the balance; education lags behind and fails to connect students to nature. Yet empowerment and transformation remain possible.

Krippner, S. The Shamanic Heart of Education. *ReVision*, *33*(2), 13-23. doi:10.4298/REVN.32.4.13-23

Modern societies, unlike indigenous ones, suffer from a lack of play. Freud characterizes the ability to play as one of three necessary for mental health. Schools are depriving children of time for play, art, and recreation in favor of college preparatory coursework. Schools can assist special-needs children by teaching techniques to improve focus, like mindfulness, playfully. Autistic children have brains that function differently rather than defective parents, as psychiatrists once thought. In this brief article, the author reviews his experiences with indigenous people, shamanic practitioners, and special-needs children. He compares the education of the shaman with that of the special-needs child in that both require a type of education that allows them to focus their attention to reach their full potentials for their, and society's, benefit.

Millay, J., PhD. The Heart of Education. *ReVision*, *33*(2), 13-23. doi:10.4298/REVN.32.4.13-23

Dr. Millay believes elementary school children must learn about the electrical and magnetic properties of their own life force using bio/neurofeedback for "Self-Discovery Science"(Self-Discovery Science is available free from: www.I-ASC.org). Children learn to increase their ability to focus attention, essential for all other subjects. Corporations, using this science, discovered ways to entrain brainwaves with the hypnotic lights and sounds of TV to exert "mind control" for increased sales and to influence elections. We are electric and magnetic beings on an electrical and magnetic earth that spins within an energetic galaxy. We are all connected in energy to the consciousness of life of the whole biosphere. This is the fundamental heart of education, and must be learned early to avoid dangerous mind control.

Ögren, J. Writing the "Stories" to Right the World. *ReVision*, *33*(2), 13-23. doi:10.4298/REVN.32.4.13-23

This article explores the power of stories. It shows how changing our inner-dialogue (the stories we tell ourselves) affects our view of ourselves, and others. There are exercises to both demonstrate the influence of stories on performance and to provide tools for change. "The Butterfly Girl," a story showing a variety of learning options, is used to illustrate how stories can help personally and be used for teaching. This story also explores differences in learning styles, to normalize and support all individuals in their quest for "knowledge." The final exercise provides tools to encourage a more healthy and creative self-image.

Santisteban, J.-A., and Lewis, L. Working with Young People in Nature: We Plant the Seeds and See What Comes, *ReVision*, *33*(2), 13-23. doi:10.4298/REVN.32.4.13-23

Juan-Antonio Santisteban, in dialogue with Lucy Lewis, explains his outdoor education work with young inner-city students in Oakland, California. He recounts the transformation of an area of neglected redwood trees on his campus into a "magic forest" where his students learn and practice biodynamic gardening, permaculture, and become aware of the voices of the trees. He discusses the difficulties of maintaining nature-based educational activities, which must compete with "academic" curricula, for student time and participation.

Sarris, G., and Perea Kaplan, C. Learning to Belong to the Multicultural Chorus. *ReVision*, *33*(2), 7-12. doi:10.4298/REVN.32.4.7-12.

All students, including indigenous ones, must be allowed to bring themselves, their subjectivity, into the classroom. When teachers act as authorities, students are silenced.

Manzanita (by Gary Newman)

On the Heart of Education: An Introduction

Cristina Perea Kaplan

Art by Julia Kate

In order to set the wider context for the perspectives offered in this issue, I provide here a critique of the loss of heart in our mainstream educational system, along with examples and suggestions for how the heart-centered can be recovered and infused into teaching and learning.

The Metaphorical Heart

The heart of education—what does this phrase imply? Is it merely a metaphor for speaking of the crux, the essence, or main task of education? When speaking of education here, we speak in particular about public education including the charter school, rather than private or religious schooling. When speaking of the heart, we speak of it in the classical sense as a place of more than emotion. James Hillman (1981/1995) tells us "One turns to the heart because here is where the essences of reality are presented by the imaginal to the imagination" (p. 28).

In addition, the heart may be seen as a metaphor for education that is holistic. It is four-chambered, muscular and powerful, in continuous polarities—activity and rest. It is part of an integrated system that works with many elements: air, liquid, mineral, electro-chemical. Yet, as a historically metaphorical organ, it has also been seen as the seat of emotion (Hillman, 1981/1995), the central place in the body: the *heartfelt* as essential, but also the antithesis of the rational. But Hillman further shows us that the heart is more than just the heart of personal feeling, the heart of Augustine (p. 26). It is the seat of imagination, of *thought* (p.6).

It is with and through the imagination, "the thought of the heart"(Hillman, p. 3), that we can reclaim, fashion, and hope to manifest broad goals for public education that are holistic, that do not divide, but connect students, teachers, and parents, to what can be known and experienced about the bodily, psycho-emotional, rational, social, mythological, and historical self, and its place in the world. Connections can be forged through education to the natural, and the constructed world, to culture, to literature, to ancestral knowledge, to one another. Marion Woodman (1985) distinguishes between solar and lunar consciousness and speaks of the heart in this way: "Heart thought incorporates past, present, and future. It

---

Cristina Perea Kaplan, M.A. in psychology, has been teaching middle school English to immigrant students for over thirteen years. Previously, she taught elementary school in a bilingual setting for twelve years. Her academic interests include hybrid identity, education, and rites of passage. She writes book reviews, poetry, and authored a mythic story that has recently been illustrated for publication. She belongs to a long-standing dream group with other students of depth psychology. Her hobbies include gardening, hiking, collage, sketching, knitting, sewing, and taking photos of the natural world. She plans to enter a credential program in school administration in an effort to help bring more balance to education.

moves in Time out of time....The heart knows what is real" (p. 144).

Origins of This Issue

At a panel discussion on education at a conference on indigenous and shamanic traditions, Lucy Lewis (2014) proposed that: "The 'heart' of education must include some direct relationship to the health of earth, which translates directly into our own health" (p. 6). Hillman (1981/1995) made a similar statement on this connection: "the evisceration of tradition takes place when the heart loses its relation with organic nature, its empathy with all things, when the core of our breast moves from an animal to a mechanical imagination" (p. 21). Glenn Aparicio Perry (2015) echoes this idea from an indigenous perspective: "The Western worldview, which psychologically separates us from both other humans and from all of nature, is ultimately untenable. To the extent that we succeed in separating ourselves from nature we rupture our soul" (p. 225).

So it is the mending of this rupture or split that must belong to the heart of education. I believe that education must do its best to be more psychological--that is soul- and heart-centered—and less sociological or centered on the needs of society. So, what are practitioners and proponents of a holistic, or as Arthur Combs (1981) discusses, a "humanistic" public education, to do? As teachers, parents, and engaged others seek to educate children, adolescents, and young adults, what skills, values, and latent talents, do we wish to impart, or draw out of them? And do classroom teachers still have choices about what, how, when, and if to teach subject matter or provide experiences for students that they find useful and beautiful?

Combs (1981) says that humanistic education "fosters acquisition of basic skills necessary for living in a multicultural society including academic, personal, interpersonal, communicative, and economic proficiency" (p. 446). John Miller (2007) believes that "Holistic Education attempts to bring education into alignment with the fundamental realities of nature. Nature at its core is interrelated and dynamic" (p. 3). If such an education is possible in the present political, and technological moment, could it not then situate the student with feet planted squarely in the earth below her, connected to those around her, and tied to sky dwellers, and to the cosmos? This issue explores how with and through imagination, creativity, and empowerment of students and teachers, this split can be repaired in teachers, school staff, in the students that we teach, and ultimately in the culture.

Editor's Connections to Public Education

I have been a part of this densely woven and somewhat tattered educational fabric for twenty-five years: twelve at the elementary level—mostly in a bilingual setting—and thirteen at the middle and high school levels. I have taught multiple subjects in Spanish and English to elementary students, English Language Development (ELD) to newcomers to the United States, grade-level English, History, and Spanish to middle and high-school students. I have also studied psychology at the graduate level in part to bring rites of passage and connection to nature to my school and district. Yet, at least for now, these efforts have borne minimal fruit. I might ask myself, why? One partial answer might be this: public education in the United States takes place, according to Peter McLaren (1999) and Cheryl Craig (2009), in a "contested" space. Many voices from inside and outside the classroom and even outside the educational establishment, vie for influence. And those outsiders, especially from within the business world, says Diane Ravitch (2014) contest for power in that space and continue to expand their reach into the classroom and influence the educational mission.

One way in which business interests influence the mission of educational scholars, experienced K-12 teachers, administrators, districts, and involved parents is with their participation in the creation of "Common Core State Standards (CCSS)." These standards, a recent educational reform, which appear progressive and initially garnered broad support nationwide from states, do not sit well with many. These include parents, teachers and now, a group of researchers from top universities, according to Valerie Strauss (2016). They flatly state that CCSS, when coupled with "high-stakes testing," diminish the quality of education. Says Ravitch (2014), a long-time historian of education, that the standards have "something about [it]… that reeks of early factory-line thinking." She goes on to say, "Stop the testing. Stop the rating and ranking. Use [CCSS] to enrich instruction, but not to standardize it" (p.18).

Common Core swept into my district approximately four years ago along with computer-based testing that required schools to scramble to acquire computer hardware at the expense of other educational priorities including arts funding, class size, and teacher training (Strauss, 2016). As business interests and leaders played a large role in the creation of the standards, they share in the largess from it. According to Ravitch: "The Pearson Corporation has become the ultimate arbiter of the fate of students, teachers, and schools" (p. 5). This situation is not a new one, but an iteration of a historical tendency.

Roots of Modern Public Education

Some would say that public education in the United States over the past hundred or more years has been shaped to an *industrial* model, the school as factory turning out identical products—in this case capable and compliant future citizens and workers (Cozolino, 2014; Freire, 1998; Postman & Weingartner, 1969; Robinson, 2015). This model is the counterpart to the mechanistic view of science that has prevailed and been explored in this journal (*ReVision*, 1999). In this model, standardized testing is mandated as a way to hold schools accountable, to maintain quality control of their outcomes, while giving teachers

> I believe that education must do its best to be more psychological—that is soul-and heart-centered—and less sociological or centered on the needs of society.

a template with which to mold students: school as factory, teacher as assembly-line worker, and students as products. This cannot be seen as the heart of education. So, the industrial model, despite its original goal of bringing equal outcomes for all students, has been discredited, according to Neil Postman and Charles Weingartner (1969).

To use a common metaphor, education seems to alternate, in pendulum fashion, between conservative impulses that wish to preserve time-honored content and methods of teaching, and more creative ones, which aspire to include new technologies, methods, perspectives, and curriculum based on educational research, social justice agendas, and culturally pluralistic awareness. Clifford Mayes (2005) deems that both of these impulses have a place in education (p. 118). In fact, according to Craft (1984), as cited by Bass and Good (2004): "the English words 'educate' and 'education' have *two* roots: *educare*, which means to train or to mold, and *educere*, meaning to lead out" (p. 162). So, the training function—imparting a set of skills and competencies to students—must clearly remain a part of the curriculum, while inborn or acquired talents and interests must only be drawn out and nurtured to ground students in their wholeness as soulful and even spiritual beings.

Let us look at another metaphor that may shed further light on the problems of education and point to possible solutions. Perhaps, as Ken Robinson conjectures, education has been more like "industrial farming" (2015, p. 41). In this analogy, large yields are produced, but at the cost of imbalance, degradation of the land, water, flora, and fauna. Education too has had much success in educating large numbers of students in basic skills such as literacy and numeracy, but also at great cost. "No Child Left Behind," a Bush administration "reform," pushed many schools to pour massive amounts of fertilizer on English and math class-es—as if monoculture crops—while taking away space allotted to heirlooms like art, music, and even science and social studies if and when they were not tested.

In addition, social and emotional skills have been largely ignored as in industrial animal husbandry, to continue the metaphor, beyond the primary grades. In the early grades, children are taught to take turns, respect boundaries, share space with a large group of age-mates. Teachers, at this level, too may feel that their cur-

Art by Carson Stringer

riculum is more balanced and heart-felt. Access to the outdoors for science, art, and other activities may be more available and encouraged. Yet, even here unrealistic standards not tied to developmental norms have begun to prevail and testing has been introduced. Free-range children may be as rare as free-range chickens!

As with the force-feeding of geese for *fois gras*, Postman and Weingartner (1969) might say, students have been force-fed "facts," rather than allowed to inquire, debate with classmates, and wrestle with problems, ideas, or stories of interest to them, that is to engage in "meaning making" (p. 91). They speak of the many metaphors for learning such as: "The 'garden,' to be cultivated, the darkness to be lighted, the foundations to be built upon, the clay to be molded" (p.91), which seem to imply that students are each just the same and merely require skillful manipulation to learn. Clearly this is not true. Theories of multiple intelligences (Gardner, 1993) and Carl Gustav Jung's ideas of typology (1971), which have found their way into personality inventories, are just two ways of looking at potential differences in styles and modes of student learning and engagement.

Problems in the Garden

By the middle school years, most students move between six or more *compartmentalized* classes where creativity and imaginative assignments may take second-place to the acquisition of testable knowledge and skills. Especially for students who find their skills lagging behind age-mates due to learning disabilities or second-language acquisition issues, elective classes such as art, drama, music, and more may be eliminated to allow for a double period of math or English taught through standardized and potentially arid texts, a paucity of interesting fiction, and zero or little opportunity to write creatively or for real-world audiences. Clearly this has a negative effect on student motivation and outcomes. And what about teacher engagement?

What happens when the teacher's heart is not in their work? What happens when a teacher or student becomes *disheartened*, discouraged? Teaching suf-

> What happens when the teacher's heart is not in their work? What happens when a teacher or student becomes **disheartened**, discouraged?

fers, students suffer from the inauthentic investment, the *half-hearted* attempts of the teacher to teach a packaged curriculum that does not engage the heart of the teacher and thereby the hearts and minds of the students. It can take a long time to realize that a curriculum that *seems* balanced and effective for a time no longer bears fruit. Gradually, it runs off the rails due to withdrawal of energy, or loss of faith in its effectiveness by the teacher who teaches it. How to re-engage the teacher, and thereby the students? Leaps of faith may be in order, and teacher empowerment that upends, remakes, or even invents a better curriculum.

Continuous efforts have been made to reform this system, such as the introduction of Whole Language, a philosophy of reading instruction, which removed phonics education from the elementary classroom in an effort to be more holistic, but which, in many cases threw the baby out with the proverbial bath water. The reading fluency of a generation of students may still be impacted. Eventually, phonics, and phonemic awareness were reintroduced, but—in the case of my former school district—with helpful components of kinesthetic learning, and personification, that is, "Zoo Phonics." This was an improvement with its multimodal and storied approach where each letter had a corresponding animal and hand motion.

Also, in my practice as a teacher and in my role as a parent, I have seen that thematic, or integrated-learning, which uses a theme, such as dinosaurs, continues to enliven elementary and secondary classrooms. It then integrates this theme into reading, writing, math, science, and art assignments. Project-based learning, or PBL (Grant, 2002), which seems to originate as far back as the early 1900's with Dewey's "learning by doing," also often includes cooperative or collaborative learning, which lends itself to relationship building—a social-emotional and practical outcome. So much that is positive and nurturing does exist, if not always thrive, in the seemingly fallow spaces in education.

The industrial farming metaphor can also be helpful in viewing the experiences of students who come to this country with their parents and who must navigate a system that is alien to them. Supports of many kinds, including specialized English-language development (ELD) courses are in place, but as with the industrial farm, the emotional welfare and cultural fit of students often

Photo by Kaplan

goes entirely unaddressed by the system, and potentially by teachers as well.

Cultural Competence and Its Absence

English Language Learners, or ELL's, face even greater difficulties fitting into a system that values curriculum and acquisition of facts over student-centered and more holistic ways of learning. They may face the issues of mismatch between their culture and language of origin, and potentially a conflict between the values of the country of origin and this country's current—and rapidly changing—sets of norms, values, and technological innovations. In addition, curricular objectives that tend toward the nationalistic or that look at ancient histories may be seen as completely outside of the students' current frames of reference. Also, they may struggle because of challenges and lack of competency in the new language and culture.

According to Carola Suarez-Orozco, Desiree Qin, and Ramona Amthor (2009), "without a sense of cultural competence, control and belonging, immigrants often feel disoriented" (pp.53-54). However, this effect may not be universal; the above authors go on to say, "immigrant girls are less likely to perceive and internalize racism from the dominant society than boys [who] are likely to develop an oppositional relationship with the educational system" (p. 58). This has been my experience with students, especially those brought up in a male-dominated culture and household. In addition, the authors (2009) discuss how immigrant youth "are constantly exposed to two sets of norms—those of the country of origin and those of the receiving society..." (p.55).

Some of my students, those who have spent most or all of their childhoods in the United States, seem to choose the route of acculturation, as I did, rather than retain a strong connection to their parents' culture—or in my case, grandparents'—of origin. In this instance, they may lose a sense of rootedness, connection to ancestors, culture, and history because they may not have the ability to root easily in this foreign soil. What would it take to allow students to maintain connection to and adherence to diverse norms and see themselves as bicultural—that is rooted in *two cultures*? Can teachers and parents value both sets of norms and cultures and acknowledge their place in setting boundaries, and caring for students?

However, norms may be seen as merely ways to control, not to empower students to moderate their own behavior. As Paulo Friere (1998) says, issues of control, freedom, and authority have not yet been resolved for many students. There is a marked tension between the top-down authority of school systems and

> What would it take to allow students to maintain connection to and adherence to diverse norms and see themselves as bicultural—that is rooted in **two cultures**?

classroom practices and the freedom and level of autonomy that students require to become responsible, whole people and leaders.

Issues of Control

Aparicio Perry (2015) conjectures that teachers "do not realize how the system is set up primarily to control children" (p. 218). And by control, I believe he means, regulating of thought, behaviors, and ways of learning. I would add that the system is also largely set up to control teachers in similar fashion. Their competence, that is ability to think, plan, and act according to *stated systemic educational goals*, has repeatedly been called into question (Ravitch, 2014, Postman & Weingarten, 1969). According to Aparicio Perry (2015), students are "the wild card"—and I would argue teachers too— that can lead to "subversion" of the system. While no minder may be watching the teacher daily, once she has been told repeatedly to teach w*ith fidelity* to a given curriculum, even a rigid one, she may feel incapable of straying off the mandated path. But, might straying off that path be the better option if fluidity and student empowerment can be woven into that otherwise inflexible curriculum?

Rightly, Robinson (2015) argues, "If you're a teacher, for your students *you are* the system" (p.xxxv). He calls for transformation rather than mere "reform" of the system (p.41), as does Edmund O'Sullivan (1999). In Robinson's view, a teacher must have the freedom, the sense of agency to affect transformation as s/he sees the need to do so, and as the results in student learning, motivation, emotional, and social outcomes dictate. Where teachers fail to interrogate or question the educational agenda and instead deliver its mandates to their students whole-cloth, then teachers and students may be caught up in an inauthentic web. It may be the students' acting out behaviors to free themselves from this perceived control that will initiate any move on the teacher's part to transform that clutching and doctrinaire environment. In this environment, can a

Photo by Kaplan

connection to nature be established, much less, thrive?

Must these transformations, of necessity, involve reinventing the wheel? Or can recent, or past examples of pedagogy serve as ideological models? Many (Hillman, 1981; Ravitch, 2014; Aparicio Perry, 2015) seem to think with Jung (1954) that the "school curriculum should…never wander too far from the humanities into over-specialized fields" (p. 51). Teachers and students may be required and may wish to make use of new technologies to enhance learning or access information, but these need not preclude timeless, holistic, and even *transpersonal* ways of learning and knowing. New technologies can be used when feasible and advantageous to learning, to student freedom, and engagement and in ways appropriate to students' developmental readiness.

Reform Education, or Transform It

Aparicio Perry proposes two popular, yet historically distant alternatives to our current bifurcated system of education: "In Waldorf and Montessori schools…the system is considerably better. There is an awareness of the value of learning directly from nature about the interconnectedness of all things" (pp. 218-219). Perhaps for this reason, Waldorf-methods public charter schools have become increasingly popular around the U.S. (Pappano, 2011). Waldorf schools can be seen as holistic and heart-centered, but somewhat rigid about avoiding the use of technology and adherence to the methods created by 19th century Austrian philosopher Rudolf Steiner. These schools include the teaching of music, art, "handwork," and writing as a later path to reading. Montessori education gives students a great deal of autonomy to choose their daily topic of study, including exploration outdoors (2018). It achieved great success in the U.S. when first introduced here by the Italian educationalist, Maria Montessori, but then declined for a time. Montessori education has seen a resurgence, of late, especially in the lower grades (2018).

Hillman (1981/1995) proposes an even more distant return to a pre-mechanistic and pre-industrial time in education as necessary to a heart-centered culture: "Humanistic education as conceived in Florence becomes a necessity again: differentiated language, fine arts, handwork, biography, criticism, cultural anthropology, manners and customs, life among things of the world" (p.113). Combs (1981), writing contemporaneously with Hillman on his perspective on humanistic education

> Where teachers fail to interrogate or question the educational agenda and instead deliver its mandates to their students, whole cloth, then teachers and students may be caught up in an inauthentic web.

goes deeper. He says "[It] gives major emphasis to the *freedom, value, worth, dignity, and integrity of persons*" [italics added] (p. 446). This emphasis must cross the power differential between teacher and student, I believe, so that an empowered and free teacher shares these values with her students in an atmosphere of *choice*.

Jim Garrison (1997) uses the myth of Eros in his discussion of Dewey's philosophy of education and equates it with an *Eros* that desires "the Good" for students without the need to possess the object of its desires. Garrison, a philosopher who writes on the relationship between Dewey and Plato, places the former within the heart of education. Garrison espouses, with Dewey, what we might now call Holistic Education: "A good education brings out the best in us. It holistically unifies our character in judgment, compassion, and practice" (p. 2). When the teacher brings *Eros* into the room, I believe that students see and feel it. Care and connection, are its hallmarks, yet startlingly, its shadow side can also have its place. Richard Frankel (1998) asserts that it has a "sadomasochistic capacity to intermingle pleasure and pain and in the process to create powerful bonds between people" (p. 141). This has been my experience as a middle school teacher!

Robinson proposes, and perhaps educators might take to heart, a new metaphor that he equates with organic farming, "organic education" (p. 44), which would operate from four principles:

Health. Organic education *promotes development and wellbeing of the whole student, intellectually, physically, spiritually, and socially* [italics added].

Ecology. Organic education recognizes the vital interdependence of all these aspects of development, within each student and the community as a whole.

Fairness. Organic education cultivates the individual talents and potentials of all students.

Care. Organic education creates optimum conditions for students' development, based on compassion, experience, and practical wisdom. (p. 45)

This metaphor and Robinson's elaboration of it strike a deep chord in me and seem to resonate with the ecological underpinnings that ground the heart of education.

Louis Cozolino (2014), whose book *Attachment-Based Teaching: Creat-*

Photo by Kaplan

ing a Tribal Classroom, is reviewed in this issue, proposes an indigenous and psychologically well-grounded framework for improving the connections between students to one another and to the teacher. As in the humanistic model, he says, "Creating a tribal classroom includes broad participation, respect,

> I have seen teachers teach, and have taught at times myself from a deeply engaged and passionate center.

and democratic decision making" (p.19). He argues that our brains have not yet evolved to learn under conditions found in industrial societies. Instead we have "tribal brains navigating modern culture" (p.29). His insights and perspective situate him in heart-centered and timeless ground.

No less than the Dalai Lama (2018) believes that "Modern education pays little attention to inner values and yet our basic human nature is compassionate.

We need to incorporate compassion and warm-heartedness into the modern education system to make it more holistic." Now, more than ever, these values are needed in schools.

"21st Century Skills"

Robinson (2015) pragmatically adds, after proposing his organic model, "But there is no denying the economic importance of education for individuals, communities, and countries" (p. 45). Indeed, even as a middle school teacher, and to a greater degree, at the high school level, students' future career goals and opportunities are not out of mind and can be one powerful motivator for student engagement and teacher focus.

Robinson (2015) also notes that the "The U.S.-based Partnership for 21st century skills" made up of state-level leaders and corporate ones "promotes a broad approach to curriculum and learning" that includes many kinds of literacy including environmental, health, civic, financial and "global awareness" (pp. 46-7). In addition, creativity, flexibility, "social and cross-cultural skills" as well as "leadership and responsibility" are listed. Robinson says that they "have always been important" and that "Many schools and educators practiced and promoted them long before the twenty-first century got under way."

But what will these future graduated citizens need to be prepared to do in ten, fifteen, or even five years as many jobs move off-shore or disappear to automation? An ecological competency, a connection to an "ensouled Earth," (Abrams, 1996) has finally begun to break through to consciousness in the national debate on educational reform. It may be the singular competency that allows humanity to endure, through improving its interrelationship with nonhuman others, the *bio*sphere.

Howard Gardner (Louv, 2008), who proposed a theory of "multiple intelligences" in 1983, eventually added "nature smart" to his list (pp.72-73). He gave exemplars of this intelligence, including Rachel Carson, who envisioned a "silent spring" if pesticide use, especially DDT, was not eliminated. But staving off future disaster or longing for an idealized past are not the answers. David Abrams (1996) reminds us that this connection must engage with and exist in the present moment, and not harken to a future idyllic time:

A genuinely ecological approach does not work to attain a mentally envisioned future, but strives to enter, ever more deeply, into the sensorial present. It strives to become ever more awake to the other lives, the other forms of sentience and sensibility that surround us in the open field of the present moment. (p. 272)

This ecological engagement can and must be made available for students inside and outside the classroom door as well as off-campus. Structured time outdoors has come to the mainstream (Posnick Goodman, 2016) as the "outdoor classroom." But, *un*structured time, e.g. mindful walks in nature, which have been shown to reduce effects of trauma, depression, and increase connection to the *sensuous* earth (Abrams, 1996) seem to be more rare, but not impossible.

Kiri Manookin (2018), who teaches English language development, or ELD, at the college level in Utah, says of her adult English learners after spending days immersed in desert parklands: "Finally, inspired, taught, and humbled by the natural world, they experience a sense of *biophilia* and ecojustice and recognize their connection to and place in the natural world" (p. 23). And they write of their connections most poetically in *nature journals*—surely a practice that can be translated to the elementary and secondary setting.

Teachers and the Heart of Education: An Archetypal Perspective

If students must be taught to build connections to nature in our ecological age, in addition to connections with classmates and teachers, what sort of teachers can help to foster those connections? I concur with others (Jung, 1954; Mayes, 2005) that one important answer is a teacher who is reflexive,

Photo by Kaplan

self-aware, and has some knowledge of psychology amongst all of the other professional competencies that are required. Yet, teachers can never be seen as having arrived, but always as growing in the profession and as authentic human beings.

Teaching has been called an "archetypal activity" (Krop, 2017; Mayes, 2005). Joana Krop discusses five main archetypes that are present in the teaching relationship: The Mother, Servant, Instructor, Hero, and Wild Feminine (pp. 55-73). She speaks of these archetypes as "healing." Clifford Mayes discusses five further archetypes "of spirit" that teachers may embody: the Philosopher, National Prophet (of "civic spirituality"), Zen Master/Therapist, and Priest (pp. 160-169). Here, perhaps we see a split between the feminine and masculine views of the teacher on the archetypal plane. But, is awareness of this perspective even partially glimpsed by most public school teachers?

In my experience, most teachers do not see themselves and their work in archetypal terms unless they have a depth psychological, religious, or spiritual outlook and felt called to the profession. Nevertheless, I believe that all of these archetypes may manifest despite the teacher's lack of consciousness with potentially positive results for students and teacher. But without conscious awareness of these archetypal grounds—even with that awareness—the shadow side of these archetypes can enter and may predominate (Mayes, 2005, pp. 170-171). "Shadow," a concept introduced by C.G. Jung (CW 9, Part 1), proposed that split-off parts of the personality, which are largely seen as negative by the ego, are projected onto others or remain hidden in the unconscious (par 44). These shadow projections often litter the middle school classroom and can wreak havoc!

Also, in my experience as a middle school English teacher of immigrant students, observer of other teachers, and a parent, I have seen teachers teach, and have taught at times myself from a deeply engaged and passionate center. This orientation feels larger than oneself, the terrain of the archetypes. When teaching from this ground, students seem to be drawn in and touched or connected to the archetype as well as to the teacher and subject matter. Guggenbul-Craig (1971) believes that it is the teacher's "childishness" that constellates the student's inner archetypal "knowing adult," and that without this "dynamic childishness," a teacher can only reach students through force, but not inspire a desire to learn in her students (pp.105-6). I find this idea intriguing.

In my own middle school years as a

> I bring curriculum to students, but I can only bring it effectively if I invest myself, my integrity into that curriculum.

student, a sexually provocative female teacher seems to have lived out the shadow of both the Mother and perhaps the Wild Feminine archetypes as she taught while wearing immodest outfits and striking sexy poses. The subject matter she taught escapes me, while her confusing and untrustworthy behaviors remain fresh in my memory. When she badgered me into revealing the identity of classmates who had damaged the girls' bathroom rather than appealed to my sense of fairness and justice, she flipped the archetypes of the Servant and the Instructor on their heads. In hindsight, she did not teach from, nor embody heart-centered ground, but rather operated primarily from shadow. Then, the effect disturbed and shamed me.

In contrast, an earlier teacher, the aptly named "Mrs. Light," was her opposite in almost all ways. A woman in her 60's with many years of teaching experience, she read us a Psalm each morning. While perhaps not entirely legal, she did not do this in a zealous way, but rather as poetry and perhaps moral instruction. She also taught us square dancing, and all of the other subjects without flash, but from a calm, centered, and caring place. I recall her frustration with my academic shortcomings, but also the sense that she saw my potential and my strengths. She taught from her own evolved culture and integrity. When she died in a fire, a spark seemed to be extinguished for me. Yet now I see that her influence and care have never left me.

In my current role as a middle-school teacher, I must constantly monitor my "culture" (Jung, 1954). I bring curriculum to students, but I can only bring it effectively if I invest myself, my integrity into that curriculum. When control over, rigid adherence to, rather than a light and responsive attitude on my part prevails—perhaps a spontaneous childishness—then I teach from the shadow side of the Mother or Servant archetype. And students do not fail to notice this imbalance. Acting-out behaviors abound!

Frankel (1998) who brings a Jungian and Winnicottian perspective to the adolescent psyche offers astounding insights. He states:

The Hermes/Trickster archetype constellates in adolescence and is distinctly related to the manifestations of the persona and shadow…Adolescents test the strength and integrity of an adult's character by knocking up against her shadow. They can sense those adults who possess a well-integrated shadow, for example, a teacher who does not need to yell or

Art by Julia Kate

threaten punishment as a way of maintaining classroom order. (p. 151)

This testing can be painful, but can eventually yield growth towards wholeness and balance for the teacher who can withstand it and integrate its lessons. Others may arrive as more balanced individuals and thrive. As Mayes says,

> Surely the health and wellbeing of young people and of the natural world are important motivators to change our current practices.

"…for a teacher to be all that he can be requires rigorous self-analysis, personally and professionally" (2005, p.115).

When we, as teachers, miss an opportunity to develop students,' identities through curriculum such as the reading of, and interaction with stories, then we function as mere technicians rather than servants of the Instructor archetype. When we miss the opportunity to connect students to the earthly, nature-based settings in literature, or the actual outdoors, in multiple sensory ways, then we do a disservice to the *"anima-mundi,"* or soul of the world (Hillman, 1981/1995).

Yet access to the outdoors remains a knotty problem for teachers above the elementary grades. Richard Louv (2008) reminds us that:

Reducing that deficit—healing the broken bond between our young and nature— is in our self-interest, not only because aesthetics or justice demands it, but also because our mental, physical, and spiritual health depends upon it (p. 3).

Surely the health and wellbeing of young people and of the natural world are important motivators to change our current practices. Teachers, administrators and parents who agree with this perspective must put it at the center of their goals for our students for a shift to occur.

Charter Schools and Hopeful Trends

The charter school movement has opened opportunities to families who could not easily afford private schooling for their children, but who desire a curriculum more tailored to their child's interests, temperament, and healthy growth (or towards the parents' desires and strivings). Arts-based schools, dual-language-immersion academies, Waldorf methods schools, technology charters, just to name a few, all attempt to refashion the mold of standards-based education and standardized testing. Yet all must show that they can meet standards through their own means. But are charter schools inherently more connected to the heart of education? Robinson (2015) discusses a San Diego technology charter that breaks many molds and with measurable successes, which include ecological technology ones. However, many corporate, for-profit charter schools spend public funds with mixed results (Ravitch, 2014).

In the case of the middle school where I teach, the district as a whole, and across the nation, indigenous, psychological, and psycho-spiritual practices have begun to be implemented. My northern California school district once suspended and expelled large numbers of students. Now, Restorative Justice Practices, based on the indigenous Maori of New Zealand and other indigenous cultures (Berkowitz, 2016) have diverted, and redressed some behaviors, and created more natural consequences. Mindfulness, based on transcendental meditation, and Trauma-Informed Care have been introduced, if not yet perfected or thoroughly internalized by all teachers nor fully accepted and practiced by all students. These practices can reconnect students and teachers with their humanity, their bodies, their breath, and with the consequences of their actions in the case of Restorative Justice Practices. But their introduction has put a greater responsibility on classroom teachers to deal with acting out behaviors of traumatized students in the classroom through restorative conferences rather than through removal and suspension. Kerri Berkowitz, Restorative Practices instructor, will discuss this topic further in an interview within this issue.

Response to Climatic and Natural Disasters

Lewis (2014) speaks of using art to "connect children and adults with their innate body wisdom" (p.6). The healing power of art became evident after the wildfires of 2017, and the trauma-inducing results of the 2016 presidential election upon my immigrant students. Coloring, drawing, and poetry helped to contain the fear, anger, and sense of powerlessness in the face of the unfathomable. Mindful breathing kept some students from panicking as wildfires glowed redly in the near distance, while also keeping my frustrations in check for great swaths of time as regressive behaviors began to manifest in many of my middle school students.

With recent natural disasters—wildfires in California, hurricanes, and floods in other parts of the country—traumatizing both adults and children, the teacher as Zen-master/Therapist archetype may need to become more prevalent (Mayes, 2005). For there can be little teaching of an unresponsive curriculum until the effects of the disaster upon psyche have been digested or at least processed in a preliminary way. Acting-out behaviors by students as well as teachers are to be expected. Mindfulness, or attention to the present moment, can help.

Concluding Thoughts

It is within the power of all us to help empower students to take on their own

Art by Julia Kate

learning in a way that authenticates who they are and what their concerns are: a responsive and holistic way of education. But it is incumbent on adults, and elders, to guide and nurture their discoveries by the settings we place students in and the subjects we introduce them to. We must respect their cultural, ethnic, linguistic and ancestral backgrounds and allow them to bring their subjectivity to the classroom, with the teacher cast in the role of guide, as they explore with their fellow students what they know, and how they know it.

And we must insure that we take them, and urge them to go, *outside* the classroom whenever and however we can. With nature journal in hand and one square meter of earth per student, observations can be made of squirming, fluttering, and waving life (Manookin, 2018). Nature games can be played, and art created. Stories can be woven, shared, and written down. As a wise person once said: What we notice, we may value, what we value, we may wish to protect. We can turn to many resources for ideas for making the outdoors an exciting place rather than a place of fear or boredom. Louv's updated edition (2008) contains a list of 100 "actions" that can be taken to connect children to nature, and questions that can be posed about the natural world and thereby to the heart of education (pp.359-390).

Others take up these ideas with clear and lucid specificity and in eclectic ways, in this issue of *ReVision*.

In this Issue

You meet authors from the worlds of education, psychology, and academia who have made unique contributions to educational thought and practice on a local, regional, or even national and international level. Dr. Greg Sarris, professor of English at Sonoma State University and leader of the Graton Rancheria of Federated Indians, brings his perspective to the issue of colonization of ethnic and racial minority students and the need for students to be "empowered disputants" as well as his own experience of education as a former student in the public middle and high schools. He also discusses the controversial killing of a local Mexican-American youth, Andy Lopez, its implications and aftermath, in a dialogical format.

Dr. Stanley Krippner, pioneer in special education, hypnosis, and much more writes primarily about the disconnect between current expectations of students and the need for more time spent in play as well as the connection between shamanism and education in "The Shamanic Heart of Education." His late colleague and friend, Dr. Jean Millay, educator and author on the topics of parapsychology and biofeedback, writes on her pioneering use of, and success with, bio and neuro-feedback

> The healing power of art became evident after the wildfires of 2017, and the trauma-inducing results of the 2016 presidential election upon my immigrant students.

machines, used with high school students to regulate their emotions as early as the 1960's, which she called "Self-Discovery Science" in her article "The Heart of Education: The Student as a Spiritual Being."

Kerri Berkowitz, LCSW, brings her broad and deep perspective on Restorative Justice Practices, which she helped to pioneer in San Francisco Unified Schools. She first came to know of it as a young South African immigrant to the United States via her interest in the use of Restorative Justice after the fall of apartheid. She has since worked to integrate it with another system of behavioral expectations known as BEST and jointly called Best-Plus. These insights are brought in the form of a written dialogue.

A former Oakland science teacher, Juan Antonio Santisteban, describes how he connects his students to nature on his school grounds in an interview with Lucy Lewis—anthropologist, dancer, and artist—who inquires about his practices. Shamanic practitioner and psychotherapist, Jan Ogren, brings an article with exercises on positive self-stories as well as sharing an empowering and beautiful healing story of her own. She uses an experiential lens to first allow the reader to dwell upon negative self-stories, then later work towards re-storying their inner narrative to a more positive and nurturing pole. Together, they could act as potential rites of passage opportunities for adults and children.

Adult and youth poetry are also offered. R.L. Boyer, poet and scholar on mytho-poetic structure, presents three of his nature-inspired poems. Identity poems by 7th and 8th grade English Language Learners from Lawrence Cook Middle School are also included that allowed students to use extended metaphor and personification to explore their identities from a rich social and cultural perspective. Student art has also been featured on our cover and within the pages of this issue. Clearly, the heart of education requires more opportunities to explore in such realms if it is going to engage and empower the whole student.

References

Abrams, D. (1996). *The spell of the sensuous: Perception and language in a more-than- human world.* New York, NY: Vintage Books.

Aparicio Parry, G. (2015). *Original thinking: A radical revisioning of time, humanity, and nature.* Berkeley, CA: North Atlantic Books.

Bass, Randall, V. & Good, J.W. (2004). *Educare* and *Educere*: Is balance possible in the educational system? *The Educational Forum, 68*(Winter), 161-168.

Berkowitz, K. (2019). Restorative justice practices: Transforming school climate and discipline. *ReVision: A journal of consciousness and transformation.*

Combs, A. (1981). Humanistic education: Too tender for a tough world. *The Phi Delta Kappan International. 62*(6), 446-449.

Cozolino, L. (2014). *Attachment-based teaching: Creating a tribal classroom.* New York, NY: W.W. Norton & Company.

Dalai Lama, H.H. (2018). Modern education pays little... [Tweet]. January 15. Retrieved from http://twitter.com/dalailama/status/952850556330033152?lang=en.

Frankel, R. (1998). *The adolescent psyche: Jungian and Winnicottian perspectives.* New York, NY: Routledge.

Friere, P. (1998). *Pedagogy of freedom: Ethics, democracy, and civic courage.* P. Clark (Trans.) Lanham, MD: Rowman and Littlefield Publishers.

Gannon, S. (2012). The crucible of classroom practice: Alchemy and early professional learning in secondary English teaching. *Changing English: Studies in culture and education, 19*(4), 423-437. Retrieved from http://doi.org/10.1080/1358684X.2012.736744.

Garrison, J. (1997). *Dewey and Eros: Wisdom and desire in the art of teaching.* New York, NY: Teachers College Press.

Gardner, H. (2006). *Multiple intelligences: New horizons in theory and practice.* New York, NY: Basic Books.

Grant, M. (2002). Getting a grip on project-based learning: Theory, cases, and recommendations. *Meridian: A middle-school computer technologies journal.* December, pp. Retrieved from www.researchgate.net.

Guggenbuhl-Craig, A. (1971). *Power in the helping professions.* P. Berry (Trans.) Dallas, TX: Spring Publications.

Hillman, J. (1981). *The thought of the heart and the soul of the world.* Woodstock, CT: Spring Publications.

Jung, C.G. (1954). The development of personality. R.F.C. Hull (Trans.) *The collected works of C.G. Jung: Vol. 17.*

Jung, C.G. (1971). *Psychological Types* (R.F.C. Hull, Trans.). Princeton, NJ: Princeton University Press.

Krop, J. (2017). Healing archetypes: Reclaiming teacher wellbeing by embodying the wild feminine. In J. Miller & K. Nigh (Eds.), *Holistic education and embodied learning.* United States: Information Age Publishing.

Lewis, L. (2014). The heart of education: A panel discussion. In conference program booklet of *The society for the study of shamanism, healing and transformation.*

Louv, R. (2008). *Last child in the woods: Saving our children from nature-deficit disorder.* Chapel Hill, NC: Algonquin Books of Chapel Hill.

Manookin, K. (2018). The benefits of nature-based writing for English language learners. *Theory and Practice in Language Studies, 8*(1), 17-28. Retrieved from http://dx.doi.org//10.17507/tpls.0801.03.

Mayes, C. (2005). *Jung and education: Elements of an archetypal pedagogy.* Lanham, MD: Roman and Little Education.

McLaren, P. (1999). *Schooling as a ritual performance: Towards a political economy of educational symbols and gestures.* Lanham, MD: Roman and Littlefield Publishers.

Nordlund, C. (2013). Waldorf education: Breathing Creativity. In R. Sweeny (Ed.), *Art education: The journal of the national art education association, 66*(2), 13-19. Retrieved from http://doi.org/10.1080/00043125.11519211.

O'Sullivan, E. (1999). *Transformative learning: Educational vision in the 21st Century.* Toronto, Canada: University of Toronto Press.

Pappano, L. (2011). Waldorf education in public schools. In N. Walser (Ed.), *Harvard Educational Letter, 27*(6), 1-5. Retrieved from www.syringamountainschool.org.

Posnick Goodman, S. (2016). Take it outside! Bring the classroom outdoors for healthy learning. *Educator. 20*(8), 18-22.

Postman, N. & Weingarten, C. (1969). *Teaching as a subversive activity.* New York, NY: Delacorte Press.

Robinson, K. & Aronica, L. (2015). *Creative schools: The grassroots revolution that's transforming education.* New York, NY: Viking.

Strauss, V. (2014, January 14). Everything you need to know about Common Core-- Ravitch. *The Washington Post.* Retrieved from www.washingtonpost.com/news/answer-sheet/wp/2014/01/14/education.

Strauss, V. (2016, March 16). Education researchers blast Common Core Standards, urge ban on high-stakes tests. *The Washington Post.* Retrieved from www.washingtonpost.com/news/answer-sheet/wp/2016/03/16/education.

Suarez Orozco, C., Baolin Qin, D. & Fruja Amthor, R. (2009). Adolescents from immigrant families: Relationships and adaptation in school. In M. Sadowski (Ed.), *Adolescents at school.* Cambridge, MA: Harvard Education Press.

Woodman, M. (1985). *The pregnant virgin: A process of psychological transformation.* Toronto, Canada: Inner City Books.

Learning to Belong to the Multicultural Chorus

Interview with Greg Sarris

Cristina Perea Kaplan

Greg Sarris

Cristina Kaplan: There was a panel at the Shamanism Conference on education and several of those speakers are writing articles for it. But, I realized as I was starting to write my introduction, that I wanted to have a Native American perspective on education, especially because this past year, I taught two students who were Native American, which was a new experience for me. And I really saw that that perspective was something I wasn't really sure of, and that it was an important thing to reflect on further, and get more information about. So that's where you came in. And I hoped that you would be willing to participate, and I'm really glad that you are.

Greg Sarris: Where are you teaching?

CPK: I teach at Cook Middle School in Santa Rosa.

GS: Oh, here in Santa Rosa.

CPK: Yeah, here in Santa Rosa.

GS: Oh great! Okay, because I grew up down the street in the Sunset apartments at West and Sunset there. So if you go down Sebastopol Road, you go back towards Santa Rosa and you come to West, to where there's a taco place, *La Fondita*, the taco truck, which is West Avenue and you just hang a right and the next right is Sunset. I lived there.

CPK: Wow! That is close. I happen to live in the neighborhood just about a mile from Cook, which is nice, but I do see my students sometimes around and about, which can be great, but it also can be uncomfortable.

GS: Yeah, yeah, yeah, tell me about it. I see a lot of my students from Sonoma State in the gym and they always come up and say, "Hi Professor Sarris."

CPK: (Laughs) You can't really be anonymous or have too much of a private life.

GS: I forfeited that a long time ago because of the casino, unfortunately. I'd love it if a lot of people were coming up to me and saying, "I read your books" or something like that but they're all coming up because of the casino.

CPK: I can see that that would be kind of an odd thing, being a professor and the whole casino thing.

GS: I wanted to do that to help my dad's people. I'm not, as I think you saw from my writing and my teaching and so forth, I'm not exactly a casino guy (laughs).

CPK: Well, that's it.

GS: I learned a lot, I've seen a lot, but it's not me.

Greg Sarris received his Ph.D. in Modern Thought and Literature from Stanford University, where he was awarded the Walter Gore Award for excellence in teaching. He has published several books, including *Grand Avenue* (1994), an award-winning collection of short stories, which he adapted for an HBO miniseries and co-executive produced with Robert Redford. He is serving his thirteenth elected term as Chairman of the Federated Indians of Graton Rancheria. Formerly a full professor of English at UCLA, and then the Fletcher Jones Professor of Creative Writing and Literature at Loyola Marymount University, Greg now holds the position of Federated Indians of Graton Rancheria Endowed Chair of Sonoma State University, where he teaches a number of courses in Creative Writing, American Literature, and American Indian Literature.

CPK: I hear you. That's one thing that I find about teaching too: you have to be an accountant with grades, and that's not me either, but the other part, that is me.

GS: The greatest thing about teaching, Cristina, and it's a wonderful thing, as I always say: Teachers and nurses, if there is a Heaven, teachers and nurses will be the first to go to that because the nurses take care of people and the teachers teach the next generation, hopefully in new and better ways. And both professions are not well regarded.

CPK: Yeah, I hear you.

GS: But you do it because you love it.

CPK: Yes, and I try to get better at it every year, but sometimes it's just so hard. My first question is about some of the efforts at reform in education, and one of them that's big right now, is Common Core. And I just wonder what you think about Common Core? Have your read something about it, or have you had some experience with it?

GS: I don't know thoroughly about its detail. But one of the things that concerns me is when you have a common core. The idea of a common core is good, that there is an equity in what is offered and expected of students—that is good. The problem is where we start to ask questions: What is the core? What is the subject? What constitutes the core?

CPK: Right.

GS: How do we know? What is the subject? And, as I always say everywhere I go, one of the big questions that American Indians, Mexican Americans, women, all of us have such a problem with in the classroom, and what the problem has been—and of course the whole Mission system is based on it—is school as a kind of colonizing activity where you are expected to put who and what you are on the back burner and adapt to the knowledge base, which is created by a certain group of people in the classroom. Those of us who succeed in adapting to that knowledge base or who may know it better going into the classroom will succeed. All of us, particularly those of us from the margins and from diverse groups who aren't represented in that knowledge base, in order to succeed we have to become successfully and fully schizophrenic because we're taught that who and what we are has no power, and that we have to adapt to a rubric that is not generated from and by our communities. So, what do you do?

And again, one of the things in the past that we've run into problems with here is that people scramble to be politically correct that is, we'll have an Indian text, we'll have an African American text, we'll have a, Latino/a text, and somehow cover all our bases. And again, you miss the point. You can very well miss the point because it's not just the subject, but how you teach it. Not everyone's Mexican American experience is the same. So when you say you have a couple of Native American students immediately I'm going well I don't know anything about them. What does that mean? Who are they? Are we thinking about kids that run around and just come out of the woods with feathers?

CPK: (Laughs.)

GS: Or more than likely, like a lot of my relatives, they're hedging in gangs and things like that. So what is the reality? What we need to do more than anything, shamanism and all that stuff aside, because so much of this shamanism stuff is really Western at heart, as I understand it, but what we really need to do is have any text, even if it's a lousy old text, and create a context of dialogue about that text so that learning becomes what it has been in indigenous worlds, in other places, forever. The best learning situations are where you're invited to bring in your background to inform the text. So the idea here is to both be informed by the text, and able to inform the text.

CPK: Yeah, I love that.

GS: And that's what has to happen. That doesn't cost a lot of money, that doesn't mean you need to bring in twenty-seven American Indian or Latino texts. It does not mean that. It means teachers being comfortable as learners, facilitating true learning situations, which are predicated, which are predicated on dialogue.

CPK: Yes, that's wonderful.

GS: So that a student feels empowered, so that, again everybody is engaged, and that way when a Latina student gets to college and takes a Sociology 1 course where the nuclear family is described as mother, father, sibling she's comfortable raising her hand and saying that definition does not suit my community where *abuelo, abuela, tio, tia* are also part of the nuclear family. And that way, the Latina is not totally colonized so that she becomes a social worker and starts yanking kids out of families when the grandmother is raising them.

CPK: I hear what you're saying. That's a wonderful answer. Today, there's an idea of kids working together in groups and engaging with a text, and then you allow them to have at it with a group, and then the teacher is a facilitator of that kind of thing, and hopefully there will be more of what you're talking about.

GS: It's not just a matter of, and the important thing here—and this often the push back that I get—it's not a matter of cultural relativism, saying that everything is okay, because, we also need to be informed in education. There needs to be respect. If you fall into the trap of cultural relativism that means everything is okay. Certain things are not okay. In some of the American Indian communities, in some of the African American communities, even in some of the Latino communities, it is not okay for men to treat women the way they do.

CPK: Yeah, I hear you.

GS: And education has to inform us that no, this is not good. So that a dialogue doesn't erode our indigenous culture, but strengthens it, makes it better.

CPK: Speaking of that, have you heard of Restorative Justice and its use in the schools?

GS: Yes.

CPK: What do you think about it?

GS: I think Restorative Justice is a great idea. But again, from what little I know of it, and I have talked to some people in this area about it, you've got people who are not prepared to really deal. It's an idea. I hate to say it, it's a liberal, I hesitate to say, a white liberal idea of doing the right thing. They don't know our people. They don't know… They get kudos for raising money and giving the Indians an orange at Christmastime like they used to do a hundred years ago.

But, fundamental change has to be in our communities. And so, if you're going to have Restorative Justice, you have to have people who are prepared to talk to our folks and council our folks, our students, and be familiar with where they are coming from and what has motivated them to fall away. Often going back to the chasm created in the classroom where they have self-alienated. There is no kid that wants to be bad or wants to do graffiti. Every kid, Cristina, is saying, "I'm here, I'm somebody, see me. They need to belong. They need to belong.

CPK: That's a very good point.

GS: And if you won't let me belong, I'll find people, I'll go places where I can belong.

CPK: I think that's part of what happens at Cook when kids band together to form gangs.

GS: Let's just create a situation here, Cristina. You have American Indian kids here and say Latino kids over there and they've had bad alienating experiences. You've got some lazy teachers around, teachers who are prejudiced or culturally naïve at best, and unwittingly alienate these students. They feel not engaged, they feel powerless; they don't feel the classroom is their home. They are made then to feel outlaws in the school. So, internalized oppression, self-fulfilled prophecy: I'm an outlaw. Let me find other outlaws who validate my outlawness.

CPK: That makes sense.

GS: That's the pattern, Cristina. I've been there. I was one of them.

CPK: That's a good segue into one of my questions or comments. You have been very open about some of your youthful activities in junior high and high school that might have kept you from becoming the leader that you are today. You mention that working at age sixteen kept you away from friends who were maybe a negative influence. Do you think work experience for even younger students, during summers and maybe some afternoons, might help students look for a way forward as you did?

> The worst thing you can do for our young people is to have low expectations. That's the cardinal sin right there.

GS: I do think that that's important. I would just hope that, and I'm going to go back to my own experience, I would just hope that students wouldn't have to be sixteen. When I began to work, Cristina, it took me away from the gangs and the streets. In fact, when I was there living at Sunset, I used to babysit for drugs.

CPK: Wow!

GS: So, some of us old folks joke about it—those of use who've survived. I would hope…what happened when the work separated me from all my friends I became extremely lonely. And I was able to see, I happened to be in a restaurant where I saw some of my friends' parents working as a dishwasher, and banquet waitresses. It became very clear to me that I was going to spend my life being told what to do by a multitude of bosses, that thought I was just a piece of—someone to wash dishes, or pick up dirty plates. So what happened is…when I went back to school. When I went back to school, it was sort of the whole Horatio Alger thing. I will pick myself up by the bootstraps; learn everything I can. Going back and learning, it was adapting to the world of the dominant culture, or the standard culture, whatever you want to call it, was totally adapting to that, and it was the most lonely, alienating experience, that I didn't come to rectify until I was a much older intellectual in college.

CPK: Right.

GS: So, I would hope that—I think work, and I think that discipline, are very important elements. And I think we should have very high expectations for our kids. The worst thing—and this is where I get mad at liberals—that just want to give them the work experience because that's what they're going to do anyway. The worst thing you can do for our young people is to have low expectations. That's the cardinal sin right there. You should expect that they graduate from high school.

CPK: That's right.

GS: You should expect that each and every one of them, each and every one of them take college prep courses. That does not mean that they have to necessarily go to college at the end. What that means, is that they're able to make a decision about college. Furthermore, they're able to be an engaged, empowered citizen of this country.

CPK: I agree. I think I had a very similar experience as to what you spoke about, becoming part of the dominant culture, and not until much later realizing what had been done to me, the decisions I had made.

GS: For me it was a real question of survival, survival at the expense of separating myself from the community.

CPK: That's right. It seems to me that your community became part of what you studied in your Ph.D. program from what I recall.

GS: And I never forgot them, I never forgot the love, and I never quite got over the loneliness. It was so hard. I don't think many people can do it. I don't know how I did it. But the loneliness on those Friday nights when, instead of going out—and it wasn't necessarily doing bad things—just being next to people, talking to people hearing stories, just being with my own people, the people who loved me. But just to sit there with a light bulb and a book was such a lonely experience. And books that had nothing to do with, very little to do with what I was familiar with.

CPK: I think you talk about that in one of the two essays at the end of *Slug Woman*, about this chasm opening when students are learning something that their parents know nothing about or have no connection to. Is that what you are speaking about?

GS: Yes, exactly. Here I was living in a home—my adopted mother was white—where I'd gone back to that home, was in a middle-class neighborhood, middle-class mostly white neighborhood—we had a couple of Latino families, a black family a couple of blocks down, but it was, for all intents and purposes, a very white neighborhood. And I went back to that neighborhood, and while my mother, my adoptive mother, was white she could not—while she thought it was good that I was studying—she couldn't help me. She didn't sit down and read poems or Shakespeare with me, she couldn't—for the life of her—do algebra or geometry. I was alone and dependent. I would imagine for a lot of our students, especially over where you are—remember, Cristina, this is not a pejorative at all—that many of our students' parents come from Mexico with a minimal education, often illiterate.

CPK: Yes, that's right.

GS: So even reading and writing in Spanish—any kind of reading and writing—I hang out with the Latino guys, my buddies in the gym and many of them are minimally educated, from Mexico, and yet every one of them has huge dreams for their children and they talk to me about those dreams. And think about those parents who are ashamed of being illiterate, and they don't want to talk about it, ashamed and embarrassed around teachers; and they feel that their kids are ashamed of them. They start joining gangs, which is not what their parents want. It's a cycle, and it'll never work, education will never work, until there's a buy-in from the parents. I don't mean the parents have to understand what's going on, I mean the parents have to be talked to and become a part of the process and feel good about it.

CPK: And you mentioned that. I have something here about, a quote of yours—it's a little bit long:

> ## But just to sit there with a light bulb and a book was such a lonely experience.

Finally, the practice of reading must work to engage the parents, and the entire community. If the parents are not involved, if they do not know what is going on in the classroom, another chasm forms across which there will be limited communication. So teachers must get out of the classroom if they are ever going to gain a clearer sense of the community." (Keeping Slug Woman Alive, p. 197).

That kind of blew me away, that statement. So I wonder, do you think that parents would receive teachers in their homes? Or are you talking about engaging with the community?

GS: It doesn't necessarily have to be in the home, it could be a neutral place, or even in the school, but become somewhat familiar. Let me just go on another contemporary tangent with the Andy Lopez thing.

CPK: Oh gosh, yeah.

GS: Police say they're over there protecting our neighborhood. Andy was killed right down the street, if you know where I grew up, and he looked like me. He had fair skin and blue eyes. And if I said to the people living in the eastern part of Santa Rosa: What would it feel like for you if you constantly had police going around and looking at every one of your children. Start imagining what it's like for us. As I said at the Andy Lopez—our tribe gave $8,000 to his family for the funeral—and I went to the big thing that the county put on. You know the supervisors were there, the congressmen, all the white folks were there, and they got up and they were saying how we have to heal and get over this, and all of this sort of thing, and I stood up—and you can go look at my speech, I think its "Discovering Andy Lopez," you can Google it—but I got up and I said to them, plain and clear, I don't understand this. You're telling us we have to heal, and we have to get over it, and all of this, but we're basically living in apartheid here, where you people are saying we have to get over it and it's a tragedy. Living on one side of the town, not coming over or understanding anything about us or how we live. And you're sitting there, saying all-of-this-sort of thing, and it sounds good, but basically I have a real problem with it. We've been cleaning your old peoples' asses, mowing your lawns, doing your dishes, feeding you…you come over and shoot our kids and then you tell us we have to get over it. What about us sitting all down together talking? What about you coming…how many of you stand in line at the taco truck?

CPK: Wow…Well, I wasn't at that hearing, and I would like to hear more of what you said. Andy Lopez was a student at my school. He was booted out for his behavior. He wasn't one of my students. But what *does* happen to the Andy Lopezes, to the families?

GS: We didn't have continuation schools when I was at Santa Rosa Middle School. But basically what happened was I just became truant. They didn't have places to put you, Juvenile Hall, so I just ended pretty much not going to school.

CPK: I hear you. That's what a lot of

> ## But the heart of education is a multicultural chorus… and the goal of education is to get us to that chorus.

our students do. So I should try to get to a couple of my questions.

GS: That's okay. Sorry.

CPK: No that's okay, I hear your passion, and I'm with you and I think I need to be more with these things.

GS: Well, you're doing a wonderful job that you're teaching and doing what you're doing. God bless you.

CPK: Well, thank you. I got my Master's degree actually in the hopes of doing something else. I wanted to do rites of passage with kids, and I have a lot of problems with what's going on in classrooms. I try to do it differently, but you kind of get sucked in to a system that can be pretty dysfunctional. So now, things are changing a bit. We can use more novels, we can be more innovative in the classroom—that's a wonderful thing, but anyway…I wanted to ask—the issue is called "The Heart of Education." What do you see as the heart of education at this time? Maybe some of this you've already spoken to, but…

GS: Well, that's a huge broad question, so I'll give you a huge broad answer, Cristina. But the heart of education is a multicultural chorus…

CPK: That's wonderful…

GS: …and the goal of education is to get us to that chorus.

CPK: That's beautiful, thank you, that's very well said. Let me see…do you remember any kind of positive experiences in education when you were going through school, that you would like to see continued or replicated? Like I think of field trips that we can rarely take now, anything like that? Or experiences?

GS: Well, my own experience is subjective and what works for me, and at the time, these days wouldn't necessarily work for everybody. But when I went back to school and began studying, which was in my senior year in high school. I was in a remedial English class and I had a very tough teacher. He was tough, and he's passed away since, but he's well known, he was a legend in this town, Mr. Gene DeSoto. And he was Anglo, and all that, but I just have to go to this: he singled me out. I felt singled out and I felt personally challenged by him. He took me aside, and he said, "I picked you out, and I'm making you a bet. Prove to me that you can do this."

CPK: Wow, that's interesting. I had teachers like that too who made me think that I could do something that I wasn't sure I could do.

GS: Well, and push you. It was like he took me to the edge and said: You're going to fall over unless you fight back here.

CPK: Wow. That's a very risky thing, I think.

GS: That is a very risky thing. That's why I prefaced what I said, it doesn't always work, it did turn off a lot of students, but he—and this all depends on the teacher too.

This isn't something that you could necessarily institutionalize. It all depends on the teacher, but I knew, I knew that he liked me; I knew that he cared. If it was a hard-edged teacher hitting me on the knuckles with a ruler or just saying: You little shit, you do this or get outta here. But he almost said: I'm not letting you out. I sensed that he cared.

CPK: Yes, that's right, and I think that's huge. In middle school we have a lot more students than elementary, I used to teach elementary, and I felt like I could care for every single student then, but in middle school, it's a more distant relationship. They need us to be closer, in a way.

GS: Yeah.

CPK: In some ways they're becoming individuals. I think we have too many students and not a close enough relationship to them.

GS: The other thing is it's that very, very—it's adolescence. And you talk about rites of passage. It's the very age where they are trying to distinguish themselves from their parents, their teachers, from one another. They're suffering all kinds of peer pressure, hormonal. All these things are, it's a very difficult age. And perhaps it's as intense as it will ever be in their life, that sense that they're separate, and different, and they're longing, more than ever, to belong because as they're trying to separate themselves, and to figure out who they are, they're aware of who they're not. And the loneliness…in this culture it is very hard because in this culture we do have a rite of passage, it's very clear: for a guy, you're supposed to screw as many girls as you can, be a jock, and have an attitude. For a girl, you're supposed to be blond and anorexic, and have boys like you. The more you're like Paris Hilton, then you've passed your ritual of passage. We do have rituals of passage, and these kids are under pressure to pass them.

What's interesting—and now I'll get back to the indigenous thing: the indigenous world, the problem of any nation-state cultures which have been in existence for about 5,000 years or so, is that we have, the culture is predicated, and depends on, homogeneity, people being alike. And so, more than ever, now with advertising and everything else, we make money by people feeling that they're not as good or can't reach certain goals.

CPK: Absolutely.

GS: We are in a huge culture where

> We are in a huge culture where the rite of passage is predicated on homogeneity, how like something, how **like** a cultural icon you are.

the rite of passage is predicated on homogeneity, how *like* something, how like a cultural icon you are. In the indigenous world, heterogeneity was honored. The more *different* you were, the more honored you were. And you were curious about it, about that sort of thing. So that's why in the indigenous rites of passage, most of those had to do with secret things or the individual is taken into a secret cult…

CPK: Right.

GS: …or went out on a vision quest, found out who they were, and learned to celebrate at this age both their separateness and their distinctness and therefore the way in which they belong as separate, distinct individuals. We never get there. We remain adolescents trying to be like everybody else and we die that way—it's horrible.

CPK: Yeah, you're right. And I think that maybe, with the Internet…I see my own daughters—I have a 15-year old and 21-year old—and they seem to want to be like certain communities, but small and distinct communities. And I like that. They have their individual quirks and such. And I hope that maybe, with the empowerment that's coming with the Internet, there can be a way to be distinctive, and fit in as well, like "nerd" culture, for example.

GS: We have to be careful. There's a caveat here, the rebel or the difference often co-ops the same pattern as the oppressor.

CPK: That's interesting.

GS: You could still have the same pattern of dominance, and who's more different according to a certain rubric or standard as somebody else.

CPK: Sure, sure.

GS: But, yes. The Internet is interesting, but one of the problems I have with it in terms of education and lots of other things, Cristina, is that it doesn't allow for deep thinking and reflexive thinking because it's predicated largely on images, not text.

CPK: That's a good point.

GS: Remember, the difference between seeing a movie and reading a book is a movie does most of the work for you...

CPK: Yes.

GS: It cheats you. Remember, a book does not exist until you read it. What happens with a book, or a longer text is it engages the imagination.

CPK: Yes, I agree... I'm trying to look at my questions here. It feels like we've gone in a different direction, which is fine. It just means that I won't ask one of my questions, but I mentioned the two students that I had last year that were Native American. One was in an advanced class, a girl, who was very bright, and a big reader. She read *Harry Potter* and different things, and was so well spoken and confident in front of the class. And the other was a boy who was in a remedial class and who didn't want to do anything. And, so it was just such a different experience with the two of them...and yet feeling like I still made missteps. I don't know where I'm going with that except I do hear you that you can't just say a "Native American" or "indigenous person" and think that it's a homogenous thing.

GS: No, and just because they're Native American doesn't mean, there's such a range of how they grow up. Many of us are mixed with Mexican, have a Mexican father in the household or a Mexican mother, or even African-American or white or others that the kids will have a tendency to go with the dominant culture.

CPK: And, actually, these two kids had a sense of their identity as natives. Like the one girl went to Pow-wows or that kind of thing. And the boy as well talked about his native roots, so... anyway.

GS: Then of course there are Pow-wows, which is a Pan-Indian culture, versus a specific California Indian culture, which is different altogether.

CPK: That's right. So, one thing you mentioned in one of the essays was the really extremely low graduation rates. Has there been any improvement in that that you've seen?

GS: Yes, yes.

CPK: That's wonderful.

GS: In my tribe, the Federated Indians of Graton Rancheria, had a TANF program—Tribal Aid to Needy Families. We don't just serve people in our tribe, but all American Indians, regardless of their tribal affiliations in all of Marin and Sonoma Counties can take advantage of our educational services. We have a learning lab with computers and all that sort of thing. We have after-school programs, we have summer programs, we have tutoring programs—all of that. And I don't know what the record is overall, what the statistics are or what affect it had overall, but I know in our tribe we have virtually everyone graduating from high school.

CPK: That's amazing. I haven't heard of that, but it seems like something that Cook Middle School could make use of for their students, for their Native American students.

GS: Yeah, certainly. And many of the families would qualify to use our TANF services and they might already be, I don't know.

CPK: They might already be and we just don't know about it.

GS: And we also have for our tribal members, scholarships and all of that. And again, the message is, you know, we have very high expectations. In fact, just last week I had to intercede because we hired a woman, who happened to be Native American, from another tribe into our TANF program and she was to work with the kids and she started talking about the Job Corps, and all these kids raised their hands and said, well wait a minute, we're planning to go to college so why are you talking about this?

CPK: Right. Very interesting. So it sounds like you talk about empowered disputants—is that what you'd call those students? (Laughs.)

GS: Yes. Yeah.

CPK: I love that phrase. Have you heard of an author named Don Trent Jacobs who goes by "Four Arrows", as well? And he has a book called *Teaching Truly: A Curriculum to Indigenize Mainstream Education*—are you familiar with the concept? And if so, what is your take on it?

GS: No, but I have an immediate repulsion for it.

CPK: (Laughs largely)

GS: Because anytime you call "indigenize education"—I don't know what he means by indigenous. There are 600 tribes in this country, all very different. And again, when you get this Pan-Indian—you get so many Pan-Indian things already, I get scared. Why a person has to call himself "Four Arrows."

> The Indians, before contact, the landscape, the features of the landscape, was our bible, was our text. Each rock, each grove of trees, each creek had a story that reminded us of who we were.

CPK: Yeah, I wondered about that too. Yes, that's why I called him by his given name.

GS: You have all these shamans who go around—shame on you, as we say in my family. You already have great traditions—explore your own traditions or mix them! The irony is when people try to become something else, they're denying who they are! They're falling into the same trap!

CPK: Yes, that's right. I guess the idea is that everybody has indigenous ancestors, but if you're Irish, your indigenous ancestors aren't Native-Americans, they're Celtic, or something.

GS: This is the thing—listen: this is what drives me bananas—I'm writing a novel about it right now—this is what drives me bananas: **you can't go back!** That's running. You're running backwards as fast as…you're still running…**quit running!** Stand right here! Stand right here.

CPK: I think it's this idea of connecting with roots.

GS: That is part of your past. You cannot forget your history. And that's what gets us dangerous. We want to forget the history. We want to forget the pain. People want to run around Sonoma County and say: Show me the Indian sites. This county is also singing with the blood of war. With the wonderful fruits and labors of Mexican families, of Filipino families. It is not just Indian anymore and it never will be.

CPK: Yes, that's a very good point.

GS: Come home, all of us, here, now!

CPK: Yes. Do you think there's a way to teach history that takes all of that into account? That isn't racist, because you have this title, *American History* and you teach it from a perspective that is colonizing in my opinion.

GS: Let's just talk about local history. The Indians, before contact, the landscape, the features of the landscape, was our bible, was our text. Each rock, each grove of trees, each creek had a story that reminded us of who we were. And reminded us of certain lessons, certain behaviors, certain things that the Coyote Creator may have done or something like that. But that hasn't changed. It's just diversified.

So there are places I go around this town—in fact I'll have Angela send you a story about *Maria Evangeliste*—about going around this town where the landscape speaks to me from my *home* past. I remember dairy farms I worked at, where dairywomen worked and took care of cows…where certain families did certain things…where life happened at Sunset and West Avenue, where I walked Sebastopol Road at night. I was simultaneously an ancient Indian and a Filipino and a Mexican and a white person all at once…all living in this place.

CPK: That's right.

GS: You have to accept people. The dialogue must be one to open us to all we are, not just one thing of what we are.

CPK: Maybe people feel like it's too complicated, they call themselves "Heinz 57."

GS: Oh, no, it's wonderful! It keeps your eyes open all the time.

CPK: Sure, sure.

GS: You know, as I always say to students and to everybody—and I may have said it to your class—there's only one art form, only one art form that America has produced, that's unique to America. Nothing in painting necessarily, nothing in literature, but something in music and it's called jazz.

CPK: You did say that to our class.

GS: But a combination of Muskogee Creek, that is indigenous rhythms, African rhythms, and European rhythms.

CPK: That's wonderful. So, let's see…

GS: Let's jazz it up. (Laughs.)

CPK: Yes! (Laughs.) That's great… there was one other thing here from *Keeping Slug Woman Alive*. So, you said:

> First, reading must engage the students in a way that encourages them to feel that they have power equal to that of the text they are reading and to that of the teacher who has given them the text to read…they must feel knowledgeable and able in an encounter with a text and when responding to it" (p. 196).

I completely agree with that, but I wonder, in your experience, did teachers just assume that you had this background knowledge with a text that maybe you didn't have?

GS: Maybe they do, but that's where the teacher has to learn to be able to ask questions, get the student to ask questions, not tell them. Have them tell stories. That's one of the things I talked about, storytelling in the classroom. That takes me out of it. That puts them in the position of the story*teller*, of the informant,

> I was simultaneously an ancient Indian and a Filipino and a Mexican and a white person all at once…all living in this place.

not me. Teachers usually become informers. They tell you what this is and what that is. All of a sudden create exercises—storytelling in the classroom is one of them—where students are positioned to tell their own stories. They become really empowered because they start seeing: Oh my god, I had answers here. That example that I gave, it's classic, where you have these Canadian Indian kids, natives. Many of them had dropped out of school, had horrible experiences in the education process, and we read something—I believe it was by Richard Rodriguez—about alienation in the classroom. And I wanted them to do something on it. They were all going to go to the library and do research, where their own lives can tell more than any book.

CPK: Sure, well that's it—

GS: —They're totally separated from, they've totally divorced their experience or any power they might have to inform the text from the context of the classroom.

CPK: Yes. Jurgen Kremer has a class that he teaches, that does a lot with auto-ethnography. And I'd like to bring that into the middle school classroom. I'm not sure about how to do it yet, but I think it can be part of everything: the reading, the writing, and all of that.

GS: Sure, yeah. I like that, where you start describing your own culture. Always reminding the student of his or her subjectivity. They don't have the last word on what it is to be Indian, or Mexican or whatever.

CPK: Yes, that's right. Well that's it because they get very frustrated with those of us who have been here a couple of generations, and who aren't "Mexican" like they're Mexican because they are more recently arrived.

GS: Yeah, "*pocho, pocha.*"

CPK: Yeah, that's it, *pocho*. What's your take on indigenous science? For example, one teacher in Oakland is having students connect with the trees on their campus in a way that seems to me kind of authentic. Any opinions on that

GS: How? What do you mean connect with the trees?

CPK: Well, that's a good question, I need to reread the article, but they study the trees, but they also go and touch the trees and hug the trees and have a physical connection.

GS: Okay, let's stop right there. How do you know the tree wants you to hug it?

CPK: (Laughs.) That's a good question.

GS: How white, how European.

CPK: Yeah, that's an interesting idea. Instead of sitting still…

GS: The Indian questioned, looked at the trees. Let me tell you what my aunt once said—I think I mentioned this in the class, I quote it often—she said, "When us Indians hear a word or hear a story, we wonder about it, we think about that story. We wonder about its genealogy, different tellers, where it comes from, what it means. We wonder about because we're going to carry it with us in our lives, in our bodies, for as long as we're alive. We don't know everything, so we wonder about it." She said, "White man is different, he don't want to know he don't know."

CPK: Wow…and so that's it.

GS: That's it—bingo. That's it…so, hugging trees: how do you know that the creek wants your smelly body in it? How do you know that tree isn't some kind of person, a medicine person that might put a spell on you and hex you? Show it some respect!

CPK: Yes, I hear you. Yeah, that was interesting to me, the story about your cousin, the hexing that happened.

GS: Yeah.

CPK: It seemed your family was willing to go all the way around it: the Native American way, the take-him-to-the-doctor-way…I wonder about the story in the Mexican culture, *La llorona*, and the Slug Woman story, maybe there's just something there that's speaking to us. The kids are always bringing up that story of *La llornona* and it reminds me of the slug woman story…

GS: And there are various ways, you look at how all the different versions and ways now *La llorona* is getting used. Because one of the old things was if you got *La llorona*—remember she mixed with the Mexican and the Indian thing, so she's punished, she's bad, and crying. So there's that version of her. Then there's the feminist version that Sandra Cisneros and others have put out, somewhat recreated, and they hate the idea of a woman crying or weeping. Then a lot of the kids use it as a ghost or a spirit that scares you.

CPK: Exactly. It's a scary story to them.

GS: So you don't go near a creek because *La llornona* might be down in the creek.

CPK: Exactly. Then there's the *Chupacabra*, that's the other one the kids are always talking about. And, I don't have that much relationship to these stories, but it seems like there may be something in them that, like Slug Woman, the kids turned off when that was brought into the classroom—some of them.

> Getting kids to wonder at the power, at the sentience, if you will, of life, of all life, not just human life.

GS: Yeah.

CPK: That there's something there that can be explored.

GS: Yeah, yeah, well that could be something…that's what they could do, remake it, use it, and always respect the story's power. That's really, really, I think, necessary. But it's interesting too, among the Mexican American people, while many of them are Catholic and see many of these things as devil-worship, or spirit, or bad things. It's interesting because, as in Mexico, they'll try—and this is very common in Mexico—they'll try the doctors and medicine, but as soon as that doesn't work they're seeking out a *curandera* so fast it'll make your head spin.

CPK: That's right.

GS: And, here, growing up I remember very Catholic Mexicans who kind of put down Indians around here, and ironically, a lot of the Mexicans had more Indian blood in them than we did. But they would put down Indians as backward, and all that sort of thing. They have that caste system in Mexico.

CPK: Yeah.

GS: But boy, I'll tell you, the minute something couldn't get fixed, the minute that priest couldn't exorcise a spirit or something they were looking for an Indian doctor so fast.

CPK: (Laughs.) That makes sense, yeah. There's that whole Mestizo thing in my family too. The Catholic thing, the European—it's like a war, an internal war.

GS: I laugh, Cristina, because all you have to do is turn on a *telenovela* to see the internalized oppression right away. The rich people all look like Germans and the maids all look like Mexicans.

CPK: Exactly, exactly. So let me see…I wanted to ask you this one last question because I'm sure we're almost out of time. Do you have any suggestions or ideas about how we, as teachers or parents, can become better role models in right-relation to Earth and non-human creatures?

GS: Um, I think just to question, or to wonder, to look at things, and imagine; to get our kids to imagine. We don't *know*; get them to imagine, get them to wonder. Well look, just ask questions: How is it that a bird knows where to go? How is it that birds can fly a thousand miles and hummingbirds can go back and forth between here and Mexico and they know where to go? In other words, what they really should be doing is de-centering us as knowers. Telling us that we're not so smart. Getting kids to wonder at the power, at the sentience, if you will, of life, of all life, not just human life. We think we're smart because we have brains—in fact we're pretty dumb.

CPK: (Laughs.) When you say it that way, knowing how to fly a thousand miles, we couldn't do it as humans.

GS: No, we can't, we can create all kinds of things. And this goes back to some of the old ideas of the local Indian creation myths. Coyote was the creator. He was a jokester. You can't trust creation. And it puts you in a position of not thinking you're too smart because you're going to get in trouble all the time. Other things have other powers. So you know, there was a time when all of the animals were people. But, Coyote thought he was too smart, and tried to kill deer, and she grew legs and ran away. She's been running ever since. Bear grew claws, birds grew wings—they're all laughing at us. We're stuck here on Earth trying to be smart.

CPK: (Laughs.) Well I really appreciate everything that you've shared, Greg, just amazing…

Created by the United Nations General Assembly in 1980, the University for Peace trains future leaders to explore and formulate strategies and practices to address the causes of problems affecting human and global wellbeing.

The Master of Arts Degree in Indigenous Science and Peace Studies (ISPS)

This program examines the traditions of Indigenous peoples of the world and their generations-tested ways of making peace and balancing societies, offering a roadmap to prosperity that respects individual and collective rights, local development models and environmental solutions.

IS IT FOR YOU?

- Do you want to help solve the global crises facing humanity by transforming outdated paradigms?
- Are you inspired to learn how Indigenous knowledge and Western science can be employed across disciplines and professions to transform crises and conflicts, and build peace?
- Do you want to spend a year studying in an academically challenging environment, at a global university with students, faculty, and Indigenous Elders from around the world?

WHAT WILL YOU LEARN?

Steeped in Indigenous Knowledge Systems and methodologies, the Master's Degree in Indigenous Science and Peace Studies (ISPS) will train you to be an insightful researcher and practitioner who understands the central issues that impact diplomacy, policymaking, and community work.

- Learn a synthesis of indigenous scientific research and theory relevant to the transformation of conflicts.
- Gain a diversity of perspectives that impact peace, justice, security, sovereignty, and reconciliation.
- Obtain detailed knowledge of the United Nations System and related institutions, procedures and instruments that affect decision-making regarding Indigenous peoples and traditional knowledge.

This course enables students to become more effective policymakers, community workers, diplomats, activists, and communicators who create change to renew life on earth.

**For more information, go to www.upeace.org/programmes/indigenous-science-and-peace.
To apply, go to www.upeace.org/pages/apply-admission.**

The main campus of the University for Peace is located in San Jose, Costa Rica

from Vajra Publications

249 pages

Available from
Vajra Publications, Nepal
https://vajrabookshop.com/

Available from
Amazon

$17.00

Transformation of Consciousness is an exploration of various approaches to impact our consciousness. The book points to potentials we as a species may need for our future survival.

Shamanic approaches are frequently viewed as premodern and thus mere historical remnants. The implication is that they are fascinating to help explain our past evolutionary history, but have little relevance for our future. When we disregard the significance of these ancient shamanic and Eastern paradigms, we disregard possible avenues to shift our thinking and our cultural practices for the benefit of our future survival.

Each author in this anthology discusses exit strategies out of the hall of mirrors that our contemporary world has created. Each contribution validates the importance of ancient traditions today, and the need for a more appropriate epistemology to describe consciousness processes.

Transformations of consciousness are needed not only to serve individual needs, but also to serve our general human need to know, understand, and make meaning. These transformations also support socio-cultural practices that are holistic, integrative, and balancing for individuals and communities.

The Shamanic Heart of Education

Stanley Krippner

Stanley Krippner

There is a bridge between shamanism and education. I have spent some time studying Indigenous people, and reading about other people's work with Indigenous people. There is a stereotype that Indigenous people today and prehistoric people as well, had a very, very hard life. It is said that they spent morning to dusk hunting, looking for food, foraging, and fighting enemies. Well, that stereotype isn't quite true.

By and large, Indigenous people spent more time playing than we do today. Yes, they went out and hunted. They picked fruits and berries, and once agriculture began they planted gardens. But, they actually spent as much or more time in recreation than they did working. And, even at that, there was no firm dividing line between working and play because they enjoyed what they did. Very often in Brazil, when I am invited to visit Indigenous people, they tell me, "We want to show you one of our games." You would think they would want to show me some of their artifacts, some of their implements, and some of their tools. No, they want to play; they want to show me some of their games.

There is a connection between the travails of modern civilization and the lack of time we have to play. It is always very discouraging to me to see how schools are cutting down art and music classes. They are even cutting down recess. They are even shutting down recreational activities, so that students can spend more time passing exams to get into college. I am not implying a cause and effect, but as the amount of recess time has gone down, the amount of mental illness in children has gone up.

In the early 1960's when I was out of high school, out of college, and preparing to do graduate work, I spent a couple of years in special education classes, working with children who had difficulty learning. At that period of time, it was felt that this was a result of poor parenting. It was believed that their absent fathers and their domineering mothers had created blocks to learning. That didn't make sense to me because I had met the families and the families did not match that stereotype. But I did notice that the children probably had special needs that were not being met in schools. Many of the children had trouble concentrating. They were what we would call today hyperactive. This was before the days of Ritalin, so the children were sent to psychotherapists. The possibilities of faulty teaching or of divergent learning styles were largely overlooked.

When I was at Kent State University, after I received my PhD in special education, we had a summer reading clinic for children who had trouble reading. I gave parents the option of letting me use hypnosis with some of the children. This was the way that I could think of helping them relax, focus, and concentrate.

I also worked with graduate students who were the tutors, and taught them ways of evaluating the learning modes of these children and gearing instruction to those modes. At the end of the summer we did a simple statistical test to measure academic

---

Stanley Krippner received his Ph.D. in Special Education from Northwestern University. He is a professor of psychology at Saybrook University, in Oakland, California. He is a Fellow in five APA divisions, and the past-president of two divisions (30 and 32). Formerly, he was director of the Maimonides Medical Center Dream Research Laboratory, in Brooklyn, New York. Krippner is a pioneer in the study of consciousness, having conducted research for over 50 years in the areas of dreams, hypnosis, shamanism, and dissociation, often from a cross-cultural perspective, and with an emphasis on anomalous phenomena that seem to question mainstream paradigms. He has written over 1200 scholarly articles, chapters, papers, publications, and books.

gains; as a group, the children gained as much in the summer school in terms of improved reading scores, than they would have gained in an entire year of school. So the whole summer school program was a success. We did this every year I worked at Kent State University at the reading clinic. However, the hypnosis children did even better than the other children. Was it hypnosis, was it the placebo effect? Was it because the parents who permitted this procedure had more novelty and innovation in their home life? We did not know, but I published several articles in educational journals so that this program would be a matter of public record. These articles are still cited. Much better studies have been done with larger groups of participants and better control groups. In general, hypnosis, relaxation, focusing, and mindfulness can help children learn better.

These studies were conducted before Ritalin and other forms of medication became the panacea for children with attention deficit disorder (ADD) and attention deficit hyperactive disorder (ADHD). From the beginning, I took the position that medication should be the last resort, not the first resort, and that it be temporary not permanent. In prehistoric times, hyperactivity may well have served an adaptive purpose in keeping people vigilant, especially if enemies and wild animals were in the neighborhood. These dangers no longer abound, at least not in the form that existed in prehistoric times. But the legacy is still in our genes.

Jean Millay has been a pioneer in the use of biofeedback and neurofeedback to assist children with ADD and ADHD. These technologies have never caught on in school, despite the fact that they provide children a way to monitor themselves, and learn how to focus and pay attention. Just as I often taught college students self-hypnosis, trained instructors can teach students of various ages such skills as visualization, relaxation, and mindfulness. And these skills can be taught in the spirit of play.

We may remember that Sigmund Freud was asked to define mental health. He replied "The ability to love, the ability to work, the ability to play." Many people remember work and love when they engage in psychotherapy, but they forget to include the ability to play. Yet, Freud felt that this was one of the hallmarks of mental health.

> In prehistoric times, hyperactivity may well have served an adaptive purpose in keeping people vigilant, especially if enemies and wild animals were in the neighborhood.

During the years when I worked at Kent State University, I not only relieved parents of their concern that maybe something they had done was creating problems for their children, I said, "These learning disability children probably have brains that are different than other children's brains and instructors need to teach them differently. As parents, you need to help your children regulate their own behavior, and assist them to focus, to pay attention, and to concentrate."

There were a few parents whose children had been diagnosed as autistic. This is back in the days when a psychiatrist by the name of Bruno Bettelheim wrote a book called *The Empty Fortress*. He concluded that autistic children result from mothers who cannot give their offspring love. They erect a wall between themselves and the child. So they are empty fortresses, there is nothing inside. Can you imagine that such nonsense was taken seriously?

Tens of thousands of mothers across the country felt guilty. They were blaming themselves for their child's autism. A few of these parents came to me. I told them, "No, you are not fortresses, empty or otherwise. Your child's brain is different from those of other children. You might say that the wires in their brain are mixed and crossed in an unusual way." They would tell me, "Oh, I am so relieved! The psychiatrists have been telling me that it is my fault."

Now, of course, we have ample evidence that Bettelheim was wrong, and not only I but many pioneers, such as Bernard Rimland were right. There was a psycho-neurological basis for autism. We still do not have all the answers but at least, medical authorities are no longer blaming mothers. And that is good news!

So how does this tie in with shamanism? Shamans are socially sanctioned practitioners who obtain information in ways not available to other members of their community. They use this information in the service of their community and its members. Children with ADD and ADHD, as well as autistic children, are not shamans. But they require instruction that differs from what is provided to their peers. They do not receive this instruction from the so-called "spirit world" as do shamans. But, like shamans, they need to regulate their attention. When anthropologists note that shamans enter into "altered states of consciousness," they are saying that shamans are using their attention to observe the world in ways that are more precise, or more global, or more inner-directed, or more outer-directed than what is utilized by other members of their tribe or their clan. Children with special needs require instruction in regulating their attention and concentration so that they can learn those academic and social skills that will help them become assets to their communities and to enhance their own self-acceptance.

In summary, the heart of shamanic education is to obtain training from a variety of sources, and these sources need to cater

> Shamans are socially sanctioned practitioners who obtain information in ways not available to other members of their community.

to the special ability of shamans. The heart of special education is to help children obtain training from instructors who cater to the needs – and the brains – of these children. In both instances, these exceptional people can assist their peers and their social group, as well as take pride in their own accomplishments once they have actualized their unique potentials.

The Heart of Education

The Student as a Spiritual Being

Jean Millay, PhD

The heart of education seems to have been lost somewhere in the midst of the ideological chaos that divides our schools, our communities and our government. How did our educational system become so far out of balance with itself?

History suggests an answer:

Our Founding Fathers valued their freedom to explore ideas. In order to prevent the mind control inquisitions brutally enforced by church controlled governments, they valued religious freedom for others as well. For this reason, all religious organizations must be kept separate from government institutions — especially public education. Because free voting citizens needed to be literate, schools, without religion, focused on teaching

---

Jean Millay Beers was born in 1929 and lived on a ranch in Wabuska, NV. 1936: Family moved to California, studied art and photography. 1952: Married Bill Mayo, helped him print silkscreen posters. 1959: Divorced. She raised their two children as a single parent. 1961: B.A. in painting from UC Berkeley. 1962: Two teaching credentials, taught art in Oakland. 1963: Taught art and English in Mendocino, CA. 1965: Won an award for a short film, and moved to LA. 1972: Demonstrated a light sculpture at the Metropolitan Museum of Art in NYC. 1978: PhD from Saybrook University. 1999 & 2010: Published two books.

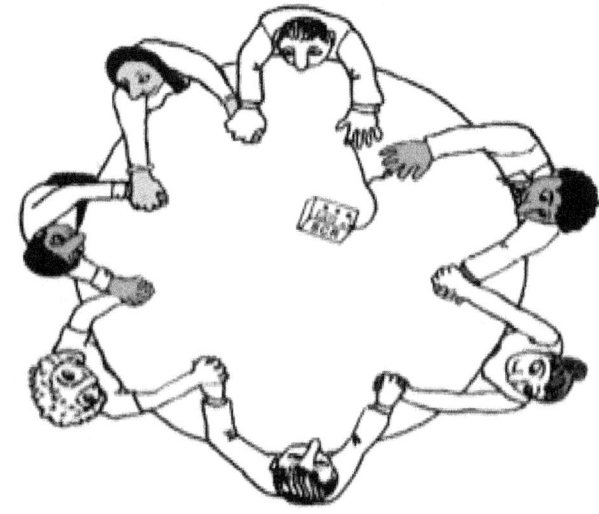

With a simple SCR machine (Skin/Conductance/Response). Students discover that they are connected electrically when they hold hands in a circle. If any one of them lets go, the sound stops. Together, they complete a circuit.

reading, writing, math and science, We felt great pride to be part of a country with free public schools that eventually included the children of all classes and beliefs.

*However, as scientific study of the material world grew to dominate which concepts could be accepted as "true," our pubic educational system changed over time. The scientific rules used to establish "reality" were very strict. If a phenomenon couldn't be measured, materialists assumed it did not exist. Materialists also took charge of measur-*ing levels of intelligence. The tests allegedly measured the intellect, logic, memory, IQ, and overall GPA, which in turn, classified students in different levels of intelligence. Those judged to have the "most intelligent intellect" eventually formed a "cult of atheist/materialism,"[1] complete with its own form of mind control. This "cult" exerted such dominance, that when well-known scientist Carl Sagan declared, "parapsychology is pseudoscience,"[2] all public supported classes about the subject were cancelled across the country with no public debate. Almost a century of solid scientific research has proven him wrong, yet the taboos are still in place, and ridicule is heaped upon scientists who dare to investigate

---

1 Stanislav Grof, *When the Impossible Happens: Adventures in Non-Ordinary Realities*. (Canada: Sounds True, Inc., 2006).
2 Carl Sagan, *The Demon-Haunted World: Science as a Candle in the Dark* (New York: Ballantine Books, 1997).

psychic awareness and heart intelligence. This mind control extends deep into the whole educational system, as art, music and creativity classes are eliminated. In righteous protest to school enforced atheistic "science," charter schools grew in number. Many rejected all science and reverted to the limitations of creationism as translated over time in the Bible.

Between the materialists and religious extremists, the heart of education—the student as a spiritual being—was lost. Neither side taught this fundamental fact: *We are all connected in energy to the consciousness of life of the whole biosphere.* Adults and children alike suffer from ignorance of this fundamental awareness of reality.

Today, children bring their different beliefs to public school classrooms. The word "god" means different ideas to each of them, and therefore must be avoided. But the words about energy connections between humans and with nature can be demonstrated in all types of classes. A child of ten can easily understand the basic fundamentals of electromagnetism.[3] From that understanding, each one can explore, through biofeedback and neurofeedback, the relationship between their own thoughts and their own electrical responses to thought. A class in "*Self-discovery Science*"[4] allows students to learn to focus attention, manage stress, and establish coherence in heart and EEG rhythms. What neuro/biofeedback, and heart coherence feedback, have to do with the heart of education is very simple. This science can open education to a wider experience of the true nature of human consciousness. It has the potential of giving the power and knowledge of cosmic consciousness back to the student and to the whole educational community.

For over 45 years,[5] teachers and therapists have proved the value of bio/neurofeedback educational experiences. I was a member of this group for many years.

---

[3] Jean Millay, *Multidimensional Mind: Remote Viewing in Hyperspace* (Berkeley, CA: North Atlantic Books: 1999).

[4] Jean Millay, (author/editor) "Teaching Self-Discovery Science with Electromagnetism and Bio/Neurofeedback" Free download at: www.I-ASC.org.

[5] Applied Physiological Feedback Association

As a teacher in several different types of schools, and with different ages of students, I have always encouraged them to explore what interested them. My job was to evoke some interest, because I had discovered that students could teach themselves more in one hour, than I could drill into their heads in a whole

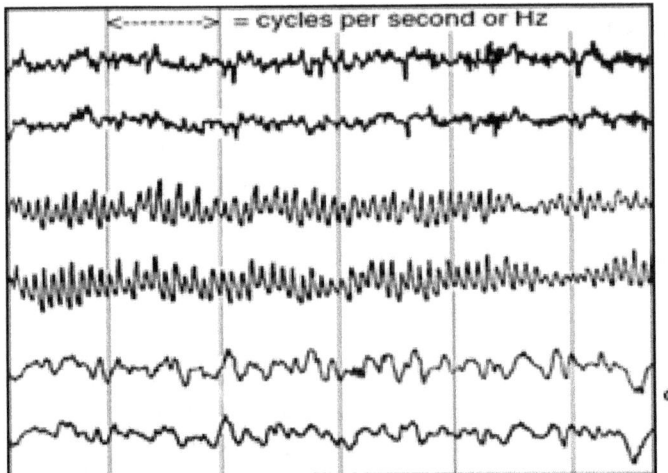

semester. Since I admit to being somewhat lazy, and not good at drilling, I decided to explore what might motivate this grumpy and rather reluctant group. My oldest sister, Marge King, was a science teacher at a Continuation High School, with an older even grumpier group. We shared our ideas and stories about our experiences, and will share them with you.

First, some background information:

In the fall of 1963, I was privileged to participate in a Peyote experience. All the rest of the major changes in my life and thought were influenced by that first psychedelic "mind manifesting" event. By 1968, I was experiencing unexplained psychic-type experiences. So, when Dr. Barbara Brown called for volunteers for her research study of EEG feedback at the Veterans Administration Hospital in Sepulveda, CA, I bravely volunteered.

Dr. Brown's lab required a room full of expensive equipment along with chart recorders to show the changes in the brain's electrical activity. This early version of a computer, costing from $60,000 to $80,000, had all of 16k (that is 16 kilo bytes, not megabytes, not gigabytes, but only 16k). It was able to sort one EEG signal into frequency categories of beta (fast), alpha (medium) and theta (slow). Brown began by scrubbing several spots on my head (ouch) in order to stick sharp gold needles into my scalp (double ouch). (Gold is the best conductor of electrical signals, and the brain's electricity is very weak.) With the electrodes on my head, I sat on a chair in front of three bare light bulbs. She asked me if I could (with my thoughts alone) turn the blue light bulb on more often than the red or green light. The blue light represented a relaxed alpha rhythm. This was at first difficult, because of the pain of the gold needles (flashing red). However, when the session was over, I knew that I had been able to control my brainwaves. That knowledge strengthened my self-esteem enough to continue to pursue my own visions, in spite of persistent criticism from others.

This potential ability to identify one's alpha rhythm through a feedback tone, and then to be able to re-produce it at will was first discovered by Dr. Joe Kamiya while he was conducting EEG research on sleep and dreams at the University of Chicago in 1958 with an ancient computer similar to the one Dr. Barbara Brown used. She was among several scientists who were intrigued by Kamiya's reports, including Dr. Elmer Green at the

Menninger Foundation. They could replicate his work, because they were already established in places where the expensive equipment was available, and could get the large grants needed to use it.

One night, shortly after that first neurofeedback experience, I had a dream about a dear friend. The next day, I was surprised when Timothy Scully stopped by for a visit. I told him about my dream and suggested that he join me to meet Dr. Barbara Brown at her lab, and encouraged him to volunteer for her EEG feedback study. Genius that he is, he had no trouble at all controlling his brainwaves. Later I said, "Gee, Tim, we need toys like this to play with. You know the government is not going to study psychedelics the way we want to study them."

The following year, I went to NYC to volunteer for Dr. Stanley Krippner's dream telepathy study at the Maimonides Medical Center Dream Lab in Brooklyn. Tim came to NYC on business, and stopped for a visit. Quietly and without fanfare, he handed me a small box with earphones, and said, "Here is your toy"—a phenomenal understatement. He had developed the very first portable EEG monitoring device ever made and gave it to me to "play" with. We were participating in an important historical event, that would one day have the power to change education, as it was generally defined then in the winter of 1969-'70.

During the next few years, Scully developed advanced versions of his portable EEG monitoring devices, as president and owner of Aquarius Electronics. He gave me his first brainwave analyzer so I could study how to design artistic light and sound feedback. We developed the first one by 1971. It used only three channels for either the right or left side of the brain. I was not teaching then, but had a job "selling furniture," Marge tried it out in her school first with interesting results, which she reported to the National Science Teachers Association in December 1972.

However, I wanted to see the patterns of electricity from both sides of the head interacting at the same time. I also wanted to see if two people could synchronize their brainwaves to improve telepathy. Scully and I completed that project by May of 1972 just in time to demonstrate it at the Metropolitan Museum of Art in New York City. This was the first Stereo Brainwave Biofeedback Light Sculpture (SBBLS).

1972 – Jean Millay, PhD, demonstrated the world's first Stereo Brainwave Biofeedback Light Sculpture (SBBLS) with the brainwave analyzers created by Timothy Scully, PhD, at the first Western Hemisphere conference on "Acupuncture, Biofeedback, the Human Aura, and Kirlian Photography" in NYC, held by Stanley Krippner, PhD. (Photo by Krippner.)

The direction of my life changed, because I was no longer motivated by my teenage dream of being an artist in NYC. This amazing "gift" — this wonderful "toy"— would teach me about my mind and psychic activity, through changes in the frequencies of different thoughts, feelings, and emotions, as registered in the brain and processed by my mind through my established patterns of memory. I had not had time to sit down with both machines until after I returned from NYC. I was playing a favorite melodic CD, while I checked all the electrodes and connections. The music (Ragas and Talas) was by Ravi Shankar and Alla Rakha. As I was settling into a steady alpha rhythm on both sides, I was electrified by the sensation that both sides were absolutely in phase with the fast rhythm being played by Alla Rakha. This experience was qualitatively different from just simultaneous alpha. His fingers must have been hitting the tabla eight times per second. Realization? Brainwaves can be entrained by music.

That is a very short version of those years, which leads into the story about how my sister Marge and I began to explore the use of biofeedback in the classroom. Marge had always wanted to teach chemistry. However, she was a single mother with four children, and was struggling with an unsupportive alcoholic ex-husband. So, she worked for years for the aerospace industry as a "literature chemist," a job that demanded extraordinary intelligence and skills. While it did improve her self-esteem, it also paid more than twice what I earned as a teacher. As her kids grew older and became a bit more independent, she decided to leave the stress and smog of LA and finally go for a teaching credential. The school that hired her was a continuation high school, filled with low achieving teenagers who were ordered by the court to attend regularly, or return to juvenile hall. When she was feeling that her early dream of being a chemistry teacher was about to be fulfilled, some delinquents broke into the chemistry lab before the semester began, and broke all the glassware. She was extremely disappointed, and wondered how to deal with such beings that hated school enough to destroy it. Steeped in her own love of science, she wondered what she might actually be able to teach them about science, or anything at all. This first story is how she managed to turn around a whole classroom of hostile juvenile delinquents. By the next year, she had students who enjoyed the "research" and her non-reading, science-hating students were struggling with articles in *Scientific American, Psychology Today*, and *Science*.

Marge reasoned that they must be interested in themselves, at least, so she started introducing them to several different biofeedback instruments.[6] She began with simple skin temperature probes, and the GSR (or SCR), which measures levels of skin conductance or resistance. When students agreed to handle those carefully, she added the electromyograph (EMG) to measure the level of electrical tension of muscles. One of my favorite stories was about a tough talking boy, who discovered that one hand was colder than the other one, and wondered why. Marge checked his shoulder, and showed him that the tension he held in the muscle was blocking the flow of blood to his hand. She showed him how to work with both relevant biofeedback machines (EMG and Skin Temp), until his hand temperatures were equal. Here is that tough guy's report:

> "My right hand was eight degrees colder than my left hand. I couldn't get either of them to change. You found a tight muscle in my right shoulder. I used the EMG and got the muscle to relax, so my hand warmed up. Later, I found out why my right hand was colder. My Dad was bitching at me, so I went to my room, because I wanted to hit him. That's why my shoulder muscles were tight. After that, I pretended I was using the temperature trainer and relaxed right away. He still bitches at me, but it don't bug me as much."

When Marge introduced the SCR to the class, she placed one person's forefinger on one lead, and a different person's forefinger on the other lead. Then in spite of much grumbling and fussing she insisted that the class hold hands in a circle. When the circle was complete, students were surprised to find that the SCR made a sound. When anyone in the circle let go, the sound turned off. When they patted hands, the sound beeped on and off in response. The energy had to pass through each of them to turn the sound on. The concept that they were part of an electrical circuit amazed them.

The unforgettable lesson: We are all connected in energy.

Recently, I showed this to an inquisitive ten-year-old neighbor. She responded instantly as she heard the sound of our electrical connection, and said brightly, *"Oh, it's a circuit."* Young people are already tuned into this type of information. It should be made available to them. The students of any age soon learn that the words they speak to each other can cause changes in the conductance of their skin. Anger or mean words cause the tone to go up, while calm pleasant words help the tone to go down. Nervous tension will increase skin conductance and meditation will decrease it. Here is a story from my 5th grade class of ten year-olds, when I was hired as a substitute for seven weeks. This class included many races and ethnic groups in a midtown lower middle-class school:

> Tom was the only one in the class with red hair. His previous records showed him to have been a "C" student. He would become extremely nervous if he had to stand up in front of the class. His parents were concerned and tried to help by enrolling him in a private drama class on Saturdays. Tom hoped to be as invisible in my class as possible. He didn't volunteer for anything. He pleaded with me to let him settle for the written part of his book report. He did not want to give it orally to the class. Again I was adamant, but friendly and encouraging. As he stood in front of the class, his face began to turn as red as his hair. When he could speak, his voice was so low that we could barely hear him, but he did manage to finish his report. It was well written, perhaps with parental assistance. His classmates empathized with his pain and applauded his success. Soon, he complained about having a terrible stomachache. He asked if he could call his father to take him home, but his father was out of the office at the time, so he came back to class. I gave him the SCR and told him to sit back in the corner of the class and try to bring the tone down as much as he could. I suggested that one way to do that would be to relax and visualize a golden light going through his stomach. During recess, I saw Tom running across the playground. I asked, "Isn't your father going to pick you up?" He said, "I didn't call him again, my stomach doesn't hurt any more."

> Months after that substitute-teaching job was over, I was standing in line at the grocery store, and noticed a small red-haired boy. It was Tom. When he saw me, he ran-up, eager to tell me that he had made the honor roll. He introduced me to his father, because he also wanted to share with us both that he wasn't afraid to stand in front of the class anymore.

A teacher might never hear about some successes. That one came as an unexpected gift that I still treasure. Another treasured success story from that same 5th grade class involved a student that worked with the EMG (Electromyograph).

Lee was a good student, though

---

[6] Some of these stories are published in "Self-Discovery Science: Using Electromagnetism and Biofeedback to Teach a Science of Consciousness." (1990) – available for free at: www.i-asc.org. Additional stories are published in Jean Millay, *Multidimensional Mind: Remote Viewing in Hyperspace* (Berkeley, CA: North Atlantic Books. 1999).

he wore thick glasses, and was awkward and overweight. Sometimes the other boys made fun of him, but he was kind and considerate. His parents were both very supportive at home. His father came to school twice a week to help students on the playground. One day, Lee told me he had a headache, so I introduced him to the EMG to relax the muscles of his forehead. After a while, his headache seemed to have been alleviated. He paid close attention when I told the class that learning to focus attention, as needed, was an important key in the process of becoming more intelligent.

Months later, I dashed into a drug store in Chinatown fairly close to where I could park. I needed some Tiger Balm for a sore muscle. I was delighted to find that the pharmacist was Lee's father. He was proud to tell me that his son had been transferred into the gifted program. After he learned to control the muscle tension in his forehead, most of his head-aches went away. That had allowed Lee to focus more on his studies, rather than on his pain. His father thanked me for what I had done for them.

These three physiological feedback instruments, SCR, Skin Temp and EMG are fairly inexpensive and quite simple to use. Ten year-olds learn very quickly how to use them. The brainwave feedback system, though, is more complex. For that reason, I was very careful to prepare them in advance to understand the concept of brainwave frequencies. We prepared them by introducing them to the Electromagnetic Spectrum Chart.

Students were eager to help me roll out twenty-four feet of lined butcher paper and tack it on the back wall. We marked off the different frequencies of the electromagnetic spectrum in order. The students were asked to choose a partner for a major project. Each team put a name in the bowl, and one student drew them out one at a time. As the name was drawn, that team chose which part of the EM chart for their project. One team chose TV, another chose visible light, another chose X-rays, etc. This project prepared them for learning about their own brainwaves, and their relationship to the frequencies of the earth, sun and sound. The students were generally quite excited to be involved in such a project, and their posters and papers were all tacked to the right places on the EM spectrum on the back wall. They could see the sequence of frequencies, and could name the differences between the VHF (Very High Frequencies of TV, etc,) and ELF (Extremely Low Frequencies). They could also see that the speed of the frequencies was related to the length of the waves — why X-rays go through you, and radar bounces off objects, etc. When all projects were done, and good grades were recorded, that is when I brought in the 100 lbs. of the World's First Stereo Brainwave Biofeedback Light Sculpture (SBBLS) that I had proudly demonstrated at the Metropolitan Museum of Art in New York City in 1972. By now they knew that their brainwaves were in the ELF range.

This brings me to a very special story that could have important consequences to our whole concept of teaching and learning and even impacts our concept of intelligence. It has to do with ADHD (Attention Deficit Hyperactive Disorder). One ADHD student was always causing disruption in class. He seemed to need to be the center of attention, and since he could not focus, he made sure no one else could either, because of his antics.

"Gary" was a hyperactive child who was wonderful at kick ball. He created a constant distraction during class, as though he were always on stage. Many of the children laughed at his pranks, others were annoyed. His reading level in 5th grade was only at the 3rd grade level. When we went to the library to choose a book for a report, Gary would only consider a story about a sports hero in large type. When I suggested another sort of story, he refused, saying, "No! Sports have to be my life. If I'm not picked up by the major's, by the time I'm out of school, I'm going to commit suicide." It was clear that he felt already branded as dumb, and his only chance of "success" in life would be as an athlete. When I announced that book reports were due on Friday, Gary complained bitterly. He absolutely needed two weeks to finish his book and to write his report. (I knew that Gary's parents were getting a divorce, and that his home was not a peaceful place to study.)

Nevertheless, I insisted that reports were due on Friday. When it was Gary's turn to see and hear his brainwaves in the SBBLS, I personally checked to see that the students had properly connected his electrodes, and sat beside him to make sure he understood what he was hearing and seeing. I then quietly suggested, "If you could learn to focus your attention, you could be a genius. Do you believe that?" He didn't speak, but shook his head, "No." So I pointed to one of the dials on the brainwave analyzer (which was continuously fluctuating between beta, alpha, theta, as I expected the EEG of a hyperactive child to do). I tuned the machine to provide a feedback tone in the faster beta rhythm (13 Hz to 25 Hz). The percentage of his beta rhythms was about 30%. I said to him, "See if you can raise the number on this dial by focusing a lot of attention on it." After that I left him and turned my attention back to the rest of the class.

When his turn was over, Gary returned to his seat and began his reading assignment. Eventually, one of the children spoke up and asked, "What happened to Gary? Ever since he was on the brain machine, he's been quiet all afternoon." Gary had raised his Beta rhythm percentage from 30% to 60%, and he was impressed with his own ability. The next day, Gary came to me with great personal pride and excitement, "Dr. Millay, Dr. Millay, I finished the book in two hours!" For the first time in his life he discovered that he could gain voluntary control over his mind. No one could ever convince him again, that he was just born dumb and that there was nothing more he could do about it.

Recently, I read about a research project by a major institution that had studied the brainwaves of thousands of children and "found" an EEG signal that would indicate ADHD. I was concerned for two reasons: 1) I knew it would be there, because I had seen it; and 2) This discovery would be used to prescribe more drugs. If those doing the measuring would even consider using EEG feedback, most children thus labeled, could learn to stabilize their focus of attention in a much shorter time, and most could do it without the drugs.

In most city schools, 5th grade is the last grade before middle school. Students have one major teacher to relate to and each student has a personal desk—a place to BE in that one classroom. If stress management has not begun for these children sooner, it should begin here, before they are separated into multiple classrooms with multiple teachers. By 5th grade, students know very well where they stand in the range of abilities as graded on standardized tests of intellectual activity. The pressure is on them, and if they are not guided at this time, unhealthy habits of dealing with stress might be locked in for life at this age. Those stuck at the 3rd grade reading level are nervous, with low self-esteem. Those who are judged to be "average" are nervous, because of pressure to do "better." And those who read at the 8th grade level are nervous, because their unique abilities are often derided through social pressure.

Responses from Marge King's high school students using this machine were very perceptive. She required them to take notes during physiological feedback practice, and write a paper at the end. Here are some comments from her students after using the SBBLS.

1) "I'm in beta when I add, I'm in theta when I'm mad, therefore I can't add when I'm mad."

2) "I'm in alpha when I float with the music, I'm in beta when I listen to the words, and I saw theta flashes on the downbeat in time with the music."

3) Beta evaluates. Theta realizes.

4) "I've learned a lot about bodily functions – how the heart, eyes, lungs, muscles and glands work. I really understand how they work. Not a textbook paragraph of which I can quote but a real understanding. I can now explain in my own words how they work in detail. I've also gained a lot of self-control and a better understanding of people. I've learned to improve my memory, how to relax, meditate, and I can identify all (practically) of my emotions."

One morning before class started, a 16 year-old boy ran in and asked to use the SBBLS. Marge helped him to set it up, and to adjust his electrodes. He watched his brainwaves intensely for a time, and then told her why.

5) "This morning I had a 6-pak and a Valium before I left home, and I wanted to know if I could still control my brainwaves. I can't hold a steady beta rhythm, now. No wonder I have trouble doing math when I do that."

I have observed over the years, that in some cases, biofeedback and neurofeedback hold a strong potential for alleviating (legal as well as illegal) drug use and/or abuse. This next story is about using the SBBLS with young adults.

When I began teaching parapsychology at Santa Rosa Community College in 1974, I wanted to explore the possibility that a person might be able to synchronize their brainwaves between both hemispheres. The Light Sculpture could only give me an indication when both sides were in the same frequency, but not when they were in "synch." So I contacted Scully again to ask him if he could build a phase-comparator for me to add to the equipment I already had. He delivered the first portable EEG phase-comparator to me just before my class and PhD research project began. The importance of phase-coherence neurofeedback is now being recognized among bio/neurofeedback therapists and researchers. Scully's machine was the first of its kind, my study was among the first, and today computers have advanced this important aspect of human consciousness. * . *

Students came from all over the country to study humanistic psychology and parapsychology with Dr. Eleanor Criswell at CSUS (Sonoma State). By then her department had two of Scully's brainwave analyzers, but students could only check out one at a time, and the waiting list was long. When they found that I also had two brainwave analyzers, some of them also signed up for my class at the Community College, or volunteered to participate in my research.

My research project involved training individuals to bring coherence to their alpha rhythms between both sides of their cerebral cortex. The following are comments from a few who participated in this first training of interhemispheric alpha phase-coherence

1) First time—after—felt clear headed all day.

2) When in Sync with myself, I have no thoughts in my head. The Synch tone is very calming and I seem to blend with it. A very complete feeling.

3) Extremely calming and centering.

4) Sustained focus in nonverbal sensuality.... The tone is on when words are absent; as soon as I tell myself about it, the tone stops.

> The present system of judging intelligence using tests that value only the intellect and memorization separates individuals from each other, and from their communities.

5) Sustained Sync elicits a feeling of being grasped in a beam of cosmic rays, an immobilization, an electric shock of energy, like being center stage in a spotlight.

In this short presentation, I have not begun to discuss the importance of the HeartMath program, though I highly recommend it. Here the goal is to establish a coherent heart rate. The research suggests that a coherent heart is a happy heart. We know that a coherent brainwave is most likely peaceful, and can in some frequencies be related to deep meditation.

The present system of judging intelligence using tests that value only the intellect and memorization separates individuals from each other, and from their communities. The present philosophy that equates higher education with higher salaries has missed the point of education. College is so expensive, that graduates become "educated slaves" to the corporations, and must "think" and "perform" according to the profit motive, rather than for the good of the society at large. Those who act according to conscience are fired. The rush to install government sponsored "high-stakes" testing, values memorization, and as teachers must teach for the test, the time to exercise reason and insight is minimized.

This flawed system of education separates each of us from the Consciousness of Life of the Whole Biosphere, though the truth is that we are all intimately connected. Each of us is alive because of our electrical and magnetic activity. We live on a planet that has a biosphere because of the electric and magnetic fields generated in the core and rotation of the planet. It is time we included that bit of information in our educational system. Brainwaves are in the same ELF frequency range as that of the Earth itself. Education must include the practice of learning to resonate in the ELF range, so humans will not continue to be limited to the mind control hypnosis of the VHF and UHF ranges of television that corporations blatantly use for profit, for the control of elections, politicians and for the usurpation of our government.

We must instead encourage free, creative, thinking for ourselves, and for our children, to overcome this new form of mind control. Teaching them how to establish coherent brainwaves, and coherent heart rhythms, returns consciousness (without any specific religion) to education. It will fall to the young people to live with the massive changes that are happening to the living conditions on Earth. Our children must develop a great deal of creativity just to re-balance those intrinsic changes that have already separated our political institutions.

Here is at least one scientific answer to the question, *"Who are you?"* You are a resonating circuit between earth and sky. Ask yourself how do you feel when you think of yourself in that way? Are you actually separate from anything on earth, or from the rays of the sun, or from the radiations from the cosmos?

> It will fall to the young people to live with the massive changes that are happening to the living conditions on Earth.

Restorative Practices:

Healing Hurts, Remediating Wrongdoing as an Alternative to Traditional School Discipline

Interview with Kerri Berkowitz
by Cristina Perea Kaplan

Cristina Perea Kaplan: For people unfamiliar with Restorative Justice, which is often called *Restorative Justice Practices* when used in the school setting rather than in courts, could you explain them? Also, would you explain the two purposes for using Restorative Justice Practices, or RJP?

Kerry Berkowitz: I'd be happy to. I see Restorative Justice Practices as extremely multifaceted in nature. RJP is both an approach and set of practices that are based on principles grounded in the traditions of indigenous cultures from around the world, that underscore the value of respect, compassion, dignity, and inclusion of all members of the community.

It's helpful to introduce Restorative Justice Practices as being both proactive and responsive in nature, although, the two are not distinct and separate from one another as the guiding principles and values are the same for both and always remain a driving force behind the practice.

On the one hand, RJP emphasizes the importance of trusting relationships as central to building a strong community in the school with the intention to foster the type of environment that students need to learn and teachers need to effectively teach. This is the proactive aspect of RJP. Examples of these practices are: co-creating school-wide and classroom values, providing opportunities for intentional relationship building, establishing a culture of circle practice, and encouraging the use of affective language which genuinely expresses feelings or emotions in relation to whatever behavior or situation may be going on.

But we also know that even when very strong relationships exist there is, most likely, still going to be conflict and sometimes really challenging behaviors that cause harm to people or the com-

---

Kerri Berkowitz partners with multiple school systems in the successful transformation of school climate and disciplinary practices through the implementation of Restorative Justice Practices (RJP). Initially working as a counselor in a middle school in Southeast San Francisco, Kerri witnessed the undeniable relationship between climate and academic achievement. Kerri served as the district RJP Administrator where she established a sustainable RJP implementation effort. Currently, Kerri serves multiple schools and districts across the nation as an RJP trainer and implementation specialist, specializing in training, strategic planning and the integration of climate initiatives. Kerri can be contacted at Kerriberkowitz@gmail.com.

munity. There will be most likely be less conflict and acts of harm when teachers and staff take the necessary time to build a caring and supportive environment in the school, but none-the-less, it's really important to have systems and a general approach that will effectively respond to student disciplinary incidents.

Therefore, RJP offers what's called a restorative discipline approach and encompasses a set of responsive practices in which behavior infractions in the school are viewed through the lens of restorative justice philosophy. One that brings everyone who has been affected by an incident together in an inclusive process to discover the root cause of behaviors as well as how that behavior impacted or potentially caused harm to someone. The intention with this approach is to repair damaged relationships and restore the community, giving voice to all those directly impacted by an incident, and together coming to consensus on a plan of action to make things as right as possible moving forward.

Altogether, RJP includes interventions such as repairing harm circles, conferences, and alternatives to suspension or expulsion when harm has occurred, as well as practices that help to prevent harm and conflict by building a sense of belonging, safety, and shared social responsibility throughout the school community.

CPK: Where and when did you first encounter RJP, and what convinced you that this was something you wanted to learn more about and ultimately teach?

KB: About 10 years ago, prior to learning about Restorative Justice Practices, I was working as a school social worker in Visitation Valley Middle School in South East San Francisco; a part of my role was to oversee a violence prevention grant which required me to pay special attention to and coordinate efforts to strengthen the climate of the school. I was invited to become a district trainer in Tribes Learning Communities, which introduced teachers to a process of student engagement and participation through cooperative learning in the classroom. This was an intensive four-day training.

One summer I facilitated three of these trainings back to back, and training after training I was blown away by the positive response from the teachers. In each training as we progressed with the content there seemed to be a gradual increase in their levels of inspiration. When I inquired about what was happening, I learned that it wasn't necessarily the content of cooperative learning that was so powerful for them, but it was the preparation stage of intentionally taking time to foster and develop trusting relationships among the students that was getting them fired up and excited.

Because if we think about it, it takes tremendous effort to reach the point where students can truly cooperate and work well with one another to accomplish a task in a small group. This is something difficult even for adults to do. It requires trust, patience, negotiation, knowing when to step up and step back, how to prevent conflict and deal with it when it arises.

It was through my experience with these groups of teachers where I came to genuinely feel the importance of school being a place of belonging for students. This is also commonly described as school connectedness which incorporates feelings of being a part of the school, that adults in the school care about them and their learning, that they feel close to people in school, have supportive relationships with adults, and that teachers and staff consistently treat them with respect.

There is no shortage of research that documents the positive impact of trusting relationships and strong feelings of connectedness on learning and academic achievement. Few would argue against the importance of the role that building strong relationships play in relation to educational outcomes for students, which made me question the reason why the numerous groups of teachers who participated in these trainings on cooperative learning communities felt so far removed from this critical component and condition for learning. It wasn't as if they weren't individually building relationships with students in their classrooms.

I discovered that the reason was because building and sustaining positive

> I realized that during the training the teachers were reconnecting to the inspiration they felt when they initially started teaching. That in order to establish an environment conducive for learning, investing time in intentional relationship building is critical.

trusting relationships was not something that was prioritized or even consistently spoken about in their schools or at a District level. At that time the messages the teachers were hearing loud and clear was only about the importance of academic proficiency, benchmarks, and standardized testing. I realized that during the training the teachers were reconnecting to the inspiration they felt when they initially started teaching. That in order to establish an environment conducive for learning, investing time in intentional relationship building was critical.

So, back in 2009 when I first heard that the San Francisco Unified School Board had passed a resolution to introduce Restorative Justice Practices, I jumped on board because the relational values and principles of RJP hugely resonated with what I had discovered during the Tribes trainings. I saw RJP as a means to truly make our schools a place of belonging for all students.

School culture is often explained by the question "When one walks through the doors of the building, what is the general feeling one gets?" The vision of our schools consistently being a place of belonging became a driving force of motivation for me. Initially it was just about students, but it quickly grew to include the adults in the school and families too.

In addition to deeply resonating with the relationship building quality of

Restorative Justice Practices, my first encounter with Restorative Justice actually occurred numerous years prior to my experience working in the schools. I first learned about a non-retributive justice approach during the South African Truth and Reconciliation Commission (TRC) in the late 90s. I followed the TRC as closely as I could and was deeply moved and impacted on a very personal level by it. Having been born into and living the first 11 years of my life in apartheid South Africa there was no escaping the impact of living in a racially segregated society, but it wasn't until some years later after immigrating to the United States with my family that I was able to learn about and feel the bigger picture of just how detrimental apartheid was for the majority of the South African people.

I think back to the late 80s when my parents (along with thousands of other white South Africans) were deciding to the leave the country. There was great anxiety and fear about what would happen as a result of the abolishment of apartheid. Many people feared a civil war and therefore decided to leave the country with their families—my family included.

Yet, under the great Nelson Mandela's leadership, not only was there not a civil war, but he very strongly advocated for and led the country towards forgiveness and racial reconciliation. Through the TRC, he challenged a traditional, punitive approach of justice and instead provided the opportunity for thousands of individuals directly responsible for atrocious acts of human rights violations and crimes to very publicly take responsibility for their actions directly to the people they harmed. This process allowed for true accountability, reparation of harms, and restoration of relationships. It was beyond my comprehension how a man so greatly mistreated and abused not only found it in his heart, but was able to lead others towards, healing and forgiveness.

I have always been very moved by Desmond Tutu's description of the TRC process. I feel his words beautifully capture the essence of what Restorative Justice is all about:

Retributive justice—in which an impersonal state hands down punishment with little consideration for victims and hardly any for perpetrators—is not the only form of justice. I contend that there is another kind of justice, restorative justice, which was characteristic of traditional African jurisprudence. Here the central concern is not retribution or punishment but, in the spirit of *ubuntu*, the healing of breaches, the redressing of imbalances, the restoration of broken relationships. This kind of justice seeks to rehabilitate both the victim and the perpetrator, who should be given the opportunity to be reintegrated into the community he or she has injured by his or her offence. This is a far more personal approach, which sees the offence as something that has happened to people and whose consequence is a rupture in relationships. Thus we should claim that justice, restorative justice, is being served when efforts are being made to work for healing, for forgiveness and for reconciliation." (Tutu, 1999, p. 51)

So when the San Francisco Board Members discovered and began advocating for a restorative approach towards Justice in our schools, I very strongly wanted to be a part of it.

CPK: I know that your training was as a social worker. Did you first practice individual psychotherapy or group therapy before working with SFUSD on training teachers and implementing Restorative Justice Practices in schools? If so, do you see a correlation or overlap in these two ways of working with individual and group issues?

KB: Yes, absolutely. Before I transitioned into the role of Restorative Practices Coordinator and later as Program Administrator for SFUSD, I worked as a school social worker for five years. In addition to working with the teachers and staff around school climate improvement, a large part of my role was to provide group therapy for students as well as some individual counseling. I facilitated numerous groups on grief and loss, social skills, anger management, and self care. Honestly, everything changed for me when I learned about and began practicing RJP. It was as if I developed a whole new set of leadership skills as I came to learn the importance of working *with* others and not doing things *to* them or *for* them. This truly transformed the way I interacted with others. I quickly saw how I was enabling the students and not empowering them by holding high expectations of them while providing the support they needed to make necessary changes in their lives for themselves.

Once I came to know how essential relationship building and creating an inclusive environment of shared responsibility was (along with gaining specialized skills in circle keeping), the effectiveness of the groups I facilitated dramatically deepened. One of the last groups I facilitated before my position changed was an anger management group with eight, 8th grade boys. I will never forget the positive impact this group had for the boys as well as myself, and I hugely attribute it to the application of restorative principles and practices.

While the content of the skill building activities were essential for their learning, I strongly believe that it was the sense of inclusion and belonging that we established together by taking the time required to build trusting relationships with one another using circles that

> Honestly, everything changed for me when I learned about and began practicing RJP. It was as if I developed a whole new set of leadership skills as I came to learn the importance of working **with** others and not doing things **to** them or **for** them.

allowed for them to feel safe enough to break through their self consciousness and let their guard down. This allowed them to enter into a zone of vulnerability where true learning, self-discovery and connection occurred.

Session after session I was blown away by the tenderness and support these supposedly "tough" and "angry" young men showed one another. In time I was able to move away from the role of facilitator and they emerged as leaders, taking control while maintaining the integrity of the group and never losing sight of the reason they formed as a group in the first place.

CPK: There has been at least one study that discusses the probability that some students project their parental issues, or complexes, onto teachers much as clients project onto therapists. When this happens, teachers can find themselves getting triggered by these projections, or respond from their own complexes, especially those who are unaware of these dynamics. As a result, many disagreements and power struggles can occur. Can RJP address these types of dynamics only in reparative circles? Or do you think that some preventative work can be done with this issue in school classrooms and teacher education programs to address this very real issue before harm occurs?

1. What happened, and what were you thinking at the time?
2. What have you thought about it since?
3. Who has been affected and how?
4. What about this is/has been hardest for you?
5. What needs to happen to make things as right as possible moving forward?

Using this approach and practice can help both the student and the teacher reflect on their relationship and what is causing the patterns of disconnect or heightened emotions or triggers that ultimately leads to power struggles.

But your question is correct in pointing out that not only can restorative practices assist when harm has already occurred, but by proactively applying the principles along with the practices it is certainly possible to create an environment in the classroom or school that could prevent such interactions between teachers and students. The inherent nature of restorative practices challenges the traditional hierarchy of power dynamics in the school setting because it emphasizes the importance of working "with" others, valuing all voices in the community, and building trusting relationships.

We can't underestimate the significance and amount of effort it sometimes takes to build positive relationships with others. Sometimes it requires a lot of work, especially in such instances as you described in your question. The great thing is that when the importance of building trusting relationships is emphasized and reinforced across the school community as it is in a whole school implementation effort, people are then given the space to slow down and reflect on the quality of relationships which would allow for one to pay more attention to the ways one is triggered by another's actions and how one's actions or responses in turn impact the other. RJP is about mutual responsibility and taking ownership of one's actions and feelings.

Using affective language is also a proactive approach to effectively communicate and address behaviors that may be triggering because it requires one to gain greater awareness of how one is feeling in relation to specific behaviors or situations and when communicated that way, helps the other person see how their actions are impacting those around them. But I find it very important to always convey that each person is ultimately responsible for one's own feelings and using affective language does not give one permission to impose one's emotions (or how they are feeling triggered) onto others; rather, it is necessary for one to take ownership of how and what one is feeling and then rationally decide if it will benefit all those involved to be communicated. In general, using affective language consistently helps to create an environment that allows for genuine and heartfelt communication.

CPK: Do you find that valuing social & emotional intelligence goes hand-in-hand with valuing the processes and principals of Restorative Justice Practices? How are they linked?

KB: Over the past ten years there has been much growth in the field of social emotional learning (SEL) in our school communities, which is very exciting to see. School climate and culture has emerged from the shadows and is now an active topic of discussion and research, and is now recognized as a critical component of the learning experience. There is a very strong link between RJP and SEL. SEL programs are very important as they teach critical competencies such as self and social awareness, self-management, relationship skills, responsible decision making, etc. These are essential qualities that aid in one's personal and social development and there are numerous research studies that show a strong correlation between SEL and academic achievement.

Restorative Justice Practices support the learning of SEL competencies through real life experience. Students gain valuable life social emotional skills through their participation in restorative

> The restorative questions are a powerful tool that fluently guide people through a process of honest sharing, respectful listening, empathy development and resolution.

KB: Repairing harm circles certainly can assist in situations where teachers and students get caught up in power struggles and disagreements. When a teacher and student come together and engage in a process of restorative dialogue they may come to better understand the greater context in which the disagreements are occurring. The restorative questions are a powerful tool that fluently guides people through a process of honest sharing, respectful listening, empathy development and resolution. The core questions are:

practices as the practices themselves (such as community circles or restorative dialogue) provide opportunities for students to actualize and learn or strengthen these skills. For example, participating in a repairing-harm circle requires one to recognize one's own emotions and the influence it had on ones actions, which aids in the building of self-awareness; or by participating in a community-building circle students are given the opportunity to develop their relationship-building skills by practicing attentive listening and being encouraged to put potential judgments aside and accept perspectives that may be different to their own, honoring each person's right to their own thoughts, experiences, and cultural identity and norms.

CPK: Is there anything that has surprised you about teachers' or students' responses to Restorative Practices when they were fully implemented in schools?

KB: Oh wow! There is so much to say here because RJP is multi-layered. It not only offers a distinct set of practices, but it also introduces a different way of being in our schools.

Truly it's been a phenomenal experience and journey for me introducing Restorative Practices to school communities. I very quickly learned that each teacher and school community will have their own unique response to these powerful practices. For some, this approach will naturally resonate for them and it

will be a seamless process of infusing the principles and practices into their classroom culture and teaching practice, but for others it's much more challenging. Introducing a relational school-wide approach into a well established traditional school system is truly a revolutionary paradigm shift and requires a significant amount of effort and resilience, specifically when moving away from punitive, exclusionary discipline practices.

I would like to say, I am surprised by the number of people who struggle with this disciplinary paradigm shift, but in actuality, I can understand. Human beings are complex organisms, change is hard, and this way of being is not consistently reflected or encouraged in our current school systems and greater society—yet.

A restorative school culture and practices help to reveal what is really going on in each moment; it calls for mutual responsibility and authentic interactions—among other things. As I mentioned before, it breaks apart the traditional hierarchical structures that create a divide and separation among people and instead encourages interactions, one human being to another, while honoring and valuing the various roles and responsibilities one may hold within the school system. This is a challenging but very necessary shift for the benefit of our youth as well as all members of the school community.

Photo by Gary Newman

Working with Young People in Nature:

We Plant the Seeds and See What Comes

An Interview with Juan-Antonio Santisteban
by Lucy Lewis

We met in October, 2014, to have a conversation. Born in San Francisco and raised partly in Mexico, Juan-Antonio Santisteban has a multicultural background, which informs his understanding of the issues his students face. He works with ages ranging from pre-school to middle school.

I couldn't help but be aware of his bubbling enthusiasm. I wanted to know how he began his work with the students at Global Family School in Oakland,

---

Juan-Antonio (Tony) Santisteban teaches science at the middle school level. In addition, he is trained in biodynamic gardening and permaculture. He and his students partnered with the local junior college in 2017 to build "solar suitcases" for students in Uganda who do not have access to electricity. His students mastered chemistry and electrical skills in order to provide lighting for these students to pursue their studies.

Lucy Lewis is an anthropologist, dancer, and artist focused on the healing aspects of art and dance from a cross-cultural perspective. She is also a body worker. She brings together art and healing in the expressive body. She has taught energy awareness to children through movement. She produced and directed "At the Hawks Well," by WB Yeats. She created mixed media videos on the *Elements, Water of Life,* and *Between Two Worlds.* These works include light projections, masks, and original music. As a student of Ruth Inge Heinze, she has presented at the Shamanism Conference for many years. Contact: lucylewis42@gmail.com Phone: 510-848-9847.

Photo by Gary Newman

California. I had the sense of his connection to nature and especially with the trees.

For the past several years, Juan-Antonio has been teaching a science curriculum to inner-city kids. It includes outdoor education, ecological restoration, and working with plants and gardens. I wanted to know how his students responded, especially to the outdoor curriculum that brought them into direct contact with nature. From a shamanic point of view, we receive much of our knowledge from nature and this principle has been left out from much of our educational system.

I asked Juan-Antonio how he came to this education work that he loves so much. He told me the following:

Growing up as a child I had the opportunity to go on group camping trips. I basically got a chance to be outdoors, and learn basic survival skills for being in the natural world. It was those experiences that created a lasting impression of Nature in my heart, and I wanted to share that with my students. It was in my late teen years, that I began to go camping with friends, and that is when I first started to sense the presence of the trees.

Juan-Antonio became more and more fascinated with the trees as living beings, and tried to understand his experiences in an environment that offered very little support.

I spent the next few years buying books and studying all about trees. Of course the field manuals give you all the names of the trees, but the names do not encapsulate the character of living beings. And I was more interested in knowing about the character of trees, so I gave up on just learning about tree classification and began to ask myself the question: What does the name truly tell me? It only tells me the family the tree belongs to, but it doesn't tell me much else.

> I began to see the rhythms and understand the forces of nature, forces that before I had taken for granted: the forces of earth, water, fire and wind.

I wanted to know the purpose of specific trees, and how it likes to be recognized in its own ecosystem. A name doesn't tell me what a tree likes, or dislikes, and it doesn't tell me what the plant's friends or companions—plants that grow with trees and complement each other—are.

I then became interested in medicinal plants and began my study of bio-dynamics, the system developed by Rudolph Steiner (1993). I began to see the rhythms and understand the forces of nature, forces that before I had taken for granted: the forces of earth, water, fire and wind.

Then in my late 20's I finally made it out to Humboldt Redwood Forest. I was astonished! Growing up around trees in the city is one thing, but seeing those giants gives you a whole other perspective on life.

It was around that time when I began working at Global Family School. I noticed that there on campus was a grove of redwood trees and I saw an opportunity. I would have the chance to share what I had experienced and learned from my visits to the old growth forest with my students. I asked the principal if anyone had ever done any work with the trees. She said no. I asked if I could teach outdoors with the trees and, to my surprise, she replied yes.

From the day I stepped foot on that campus, those trees felt familiar to me. Do you know how it is, when you see someone you haven't seen for a while, and you can catch up right where you left off? It was like that with the trees at school. They were telling me they missed the children. Unfortunately the section of the yard where the trees lived had been blocked off to serve as a parking lot for the staff. So the trees had lost contact with the children.

I first started taking the kids out to the grove to hug the trees and gently climb on them too. I would take my classes out there for the sake of providing my students time with nature. I would tell them that we were going to start working with the land. But in order to get started they needed to begin to recognize the trees as living beings that were as alive as they were. We first began by saying hello to the trees as a way of showing respect and recognition to our tree friends.

Then it took off from there; we had a single redwood tree in the lower yard of the school that became a whole ritual. The kids started to ask things like, "Can we hold hands around the tree?" and I would say, "That's a great idea!" We did that for about a year, and the students really liked the time they were spending with the trees, so I began to embed this time into the curriculum calling it, "Redwood Exploration Time."

The principal liked what I was doing and fenced off the redwood area the following school year, so that we could have an area designated as an outdoor classroom. That year we began studying California state parks and their history, and focusing on conservation groups like "Save the Redwoods League," and those who stood up for the protection of nature. I introduced them to the National Geographic video, "Climbing Redwood Giants." As they began to explore the history of redwoods, a sense of stewardship began to grow within the students. They would ask, "What are we going to do Mr. S? We have got to save the trees!"

Important to trees is water and healthy soil, so we wanted to start there, but first we had to clean the area up. But, no matter how hard we tried the parents would continue to leave trash around the trees. Every day was a new mess, so the kids said, "Let's make signs. Let's make signs to protect the area." And they did; they put their signs all around the center tree. And the trash began to lessen significantly.

Outside of work, I was continuing my studies of horticulture and permaculture at Merritt College. I also got the chance to take a workshop at the Rudolf Steiner College for deeper understanding of biodynamics. I began to understand more about plant life as a living consciousness, I felt responsible to help the other trees on the campus.

> I began to understand more about plant life as a living consciousness.

An Example of How a Good Idea Can Go Wrong

Over time I began meeting with the landscaping people for the district, and found out that they wanted to go have a gardener come to the school and prune some of the trees by using an approach that was not sensitive to the land. So I asked, if I could be there when they came by in order to help with the pruning. They said I could, but schedules changed and they came on a day when I was not there. They ended up chopping down four Australian bottlebrush trees to barely a nub, just enough to be able to grow back.

Now what they didn't know was that the four trees they cut were the main sources of food for our local hummingbirds. How did the students feel about this? There would be days when I would take the kids out there and we would just sit; we would be quiet and just sit and look at the hummingbirds, watch the butterflies, and the bees. You would think that would be hard to do with kids, being quiet for so long. But because we had been spending the time there they could sense the magic of that place, and it became the magical forest.

They would bring up characters from stories I would tell them, and now there was Spirit Bear and Sitting Deer as members of the magical forest; in the same way the trees were a part of the school, these characters were now a part of the forest. The kids would use their imagination and they would say things like, "I saw Spirit Bear and he was telling me to come over and look behind the tree, and he was telling me we have to cover this area with mulch." And I'd say, "Okay, let's."

As I became aware that the kids were becoming more sensitive to the land, I wanted to show them how to help our redwood trees. At that time the trees didn't show signs of being healthy, the ground was bare, dry and the trees didn't even have fairy rings around the base (a group of young starts that surround the base of the trunk of healthy redwood trees). I connected with the city to collect compost, and they dropped off about 10 cubic feet of it on the school driveway. The kids along with a colleague and I started shoveling and moving it onto the redwoods.

Slowly it began bringing the vitality back to the land and turning it into living mulch for our small forest. It took about a year and a half of dedicated work on the part of the students, and this year the trees began giving sprouts, forming their very first fairy rings. Showing the students how to heal the land, and teaching them how to create the living conditions the redwood trees needed to thrive, was amazing. This type of education with nature needs to be reproduced in the public sector.

I asked my students questions like: What do you think the redwood tree likes?

Then we would start a discussion on what the trees might like, and the amount of water they preferred to have. We talked about temperate rain forests, which is the type of forest our kind of redwood belongs to. It is actually the type of climate these trees create as they begin to spread out over long periods of time.

Unlike other trees, the costal redwood creates its own environment. This makes redwoods so unbelievable. Their roots spread out and connect with other redwoods, so that they support themselves by their relationship to each other. These are principles that can teach kids about themselves.

Last year one of our redwood trees started giving seeds. We took some of those seeds and studied them under a magnifying glass; we even tried to grow the trees from seeds. Though none of the seeds grew, the students learned that it is difficult to grow redwoods from seeds. They learned that redwoods typically propagate through burls, which is why young starts around the base of the trunk are important for redwood trees. Students would ask, "Is this a mama tree or a papa tree?" and learned that redwood trees are actually both. Redwoods have two sets of leaves, male and female leaves on the same tree.

During the typical school week students are pressed to learn for long periods of time sitting down, and are tested endlessly. So when they come to my class for their science period, I try to encourage the students to get closer to nature and be outside. During my lessons I try not to talk too much and I guide the lessons by asking them questions. As they ask me questions, I don't answer them all, instead I turn it back to them, so that they can answer their own questions. In the process they develop confidence in their own abilities.

For example, in the after-school program that I teach, I noticed that the kids didn't want to leave. If their parents pick them up early, the students are actually sad. That tells me that they are engaged and feel confident with the work they do for the land. They look forward to Fridays and it always amazes me how children have a natural soft spot for nature.

The original outlook changed when we got a new principal. The district-mandated classroom academic minutes once again began to challenge the outdoor program.

> Their roots spread out and connect with other Redwoods, so that they support themselves by their relationship to each other. These are principles that can teach kids about themselves.

> This work helps open up pathways to deeper connections and understandings, which is my main goal during outdoor education time.

But when our school won a recycling competition through the district, our principal changed his mind about the program and Eco-stewardship education was back!

The recycling competition made the local news; cameras came out to the school because our school had achieved major trash reduction: only four percent of our school waste was going to the landfill. We now had compost bins at our school for the first time.

At this point, I introduced biodynamic gardening and permaculture into the curriculum. I want to give our inner city kids an opportunity to have a redwood forest, to restore, preserve and protect the land so they understand the relationship between humans, plants, trees and other beings. This work helps open up pathways to deeper connections and understandings, which is my main goal during outdoor education time. You don't need to get caught up thinking of what comes next, when you know how to appreciate being in the moment.

Our principal is going to give us a small budget to purchase plants for a permaculture design. We can now begin to help restore the redwoods ecosystem. We also have a small vegetable garden in the upper yard of the school, including a 4'x5' strawberry bed maintained by students and colleagues who also work hard to make outdoor experiences happen for our students.

Just yesterday I met with the landscape department for the district, because yet another teacher concerned about lawn maintenance. But I found alternative locations and it looks like we will soon have twelve new garden beds.

The garden is symbolic for humans; it represents us, awakening to what is possible. The outlook now is to strive for all the teachers to have a garden area, making it possible to teach a garden curriculum in the redwood forest. I can see that the soil in our small forest is healthy enough that it will be possible to grow food in that area. A few years ago it wouldn't have been possible to grow food, because of the poor soil conditions. I think we can do it now, and with a small budget we will soon have a garden in the redwoods. We have this new opportunity to create a healing garden, a place for learning from and experiencing nature.

I have informally been giving instruction to other teachers who want to do the same kind of work. Over this past summer I had the opportunity to teach a curriculum on habitats. I loved the chance to share this type of information with kids. I feel like I would do this whether I was getting paid or not, and I am learning to live every day with less and less.

Eventually I want to own a farm where I can practice biodynamic farming. In a way, biodynamic gardening and permaculture set the basis for learning to live with other beings because of the connection between nature and us. Why are we shy to say that plants and the soil are other living beings? They are not human beings, but they are living beings nonetheless that need to be recognized and given more than just a name.

From permaculture, I have learned that there is this magic that takes over a designed garden after four or five years. Once you begin to bring these plant beings together, they now have an actual place to live and grow, a place they can call home. That magic happens because everything is now in balance. You

> Do you have to think about your heartbeat at all times of the day? The same spirit that embodies us embodies everything.

can harvest what comes from the garden, and the system sustains itself and will regenerate. Do you have to think about your heartbeat at all times of the day? The same spirit that embodies us embodies everything.

That is the cool part, to be able to describe the magic that happens to the students, the process as a living being known as *Pachamama*. Now, the kids greet the Earth as *Pachamama*. We are giving it not just a name, but also a sense of being.

At first the students would say, "Mr. S, rocks aren't alive," but by the time they get to 4th grade they learn about the rock cycle. How could a rock not be alive if it is constantly in motion, changing and reinventing itself? The inclusion of outdoor education along with the school curriculum helps deepen the understanding and connections to the concepts kids are learning.

I have been bringing in music; the kids call the music "native jams;" they are songs from South America. The younger kids love to chant and march around the tree. They sing, "We love Mother Earth." This came out of them; I didn't even suggest it. Another chant they created was "Heal the Earth." It just came from them, and it is such a positive feeling to see this happen.

I feel that the best way I can share my teaching experiences, as far as an instructional model goes, would be to record the experiences

> Why are we shy to say that plants and the soil are other living beings?

showed interest in gardening, making twelve teachers who now want a garden plot. I am grateful to my colleagues for striving just as hard to support eco-stewardship. But the prime sun location at the school has a giant lawn and we can't use that space because the district is and let other instructors apply this material in their own way. Even if you have an administration that is opposed to outdoor education, once they see the way the kids gravitate towards nature and they see a deeper enthusiasm coming from the students, that will speak for itself.

The biggest challenge for me has been the opposition from colleagues and administration to our outdoor time, which they do not consider as academic instructional minutes. My school has not always been supportive of a nature-based education, however things are changing, and Next Generation Science Standards (NGSS) are now becoming more open about outdoor learning, and for that I am grateful.

I asked Juan-Antonio how he could see his work expanding into a broader curriculum and what he felt needed to be done to get more support.

One way of enriching the curriculum is with storytelling. I tell stories, but I would like to invite more storytellers into our forest. It is one thing to hear me tell stories, but to hear them from other adults would help broaden their imagination to the magic of nature. The beautiful stories I heard at the Society for the Study of Shamanism, Healing and Transformation Conference were so bright and filled with light that I would love to bring that type of storytelling to our forest.

We Plant the Seeds and See What Comes Up

We are in the process of starting a medicinal herb garden, and we are growing our plants without chemicals or fertilizers. And to think, this is taking place here in Oakland, California where kids do not have much contact with nature. This year I am pushing for more parent involvement to assist with our Redwood restoration project.

If you are interested in contacting Juan-Antonio Santisteban about his project, please contact him at Juan-Antonio (Tony) Santisteban, emc2isgod@hotmail.com

References

Elpel, T. (2004). *Botany in a day: The patterns method of plant identification.* Pony, MT: HOPS Press, LLC.

Ingam, E. (2000). *Soil Biology Primer.* Ankeny, IA: Soil and Water Conservation Society.

Kershner, B. (2008*). National Wildlife Federation field guide to trees of North America.* Boston, MA: Chanticleer Press, Inc.

Matthias, T. (2019). *The North American Maria Thun Biodynamic Sowing and Planting Calendar.* (B. Jarman, Trans.). Edinburgh, Scotland.

Morrow, R. (2006). *Earth user's guide to permaculture* (2nd ed.). Pymble, Australia: Kangaroo Press.

National Geographic Society (Producer) (2009). "Climbing Redwood Giants." [Video].

Steiner, R. (1993). *Agriculture: Spiritual foundations for the renewal of agriculture* (7th ed.) Junction City, OR: Biodynamic Farming and Gardening Association.

Tomkins, P. & Bird, C. (1998). Secrets of the soil: New solutions for restoring our planet. Anchorage, AK: Earthpulse Press.

Texts by Youth: Poems on Identity

7th and 8th Grade ELD* Students of Lawrence Cook Middle School

Photos by Kaplan

I'm a blue spiral
stretching and jumping,

I'm the growl of a cheetah stalking its prey,

I'm "Starship" played on the radio,

I'm a black Lamborghini cruising down the highway,

I'm a tan bed covered with pillows,

I'm a hot taco covered with chile,

I'm a beautiful palm tree standing on the beach,

I'm a loud drum played by a band,

I'm a scary snake rolled on a tree,

I'm hot Apatzingen, Michoacan,

I'm a YOLO having fun…

—MLJ

I'm a red rhombus
jumping and stretching,

I'm a shark stalking its prey,

I'm "Eres mi necesidad" played on the computer,

I'm a black Hummer cruising down the highway,

I'm a red chair covered with pillows,

I'm a delicious pizza covered with cheese,

I'm a raging volcano pouring out lava in Hawaii,

I'm a good-looking pine standing in the university,

I'm a new guitar played in the house,

I'm a venomous spider creeping in a desert,

I'm Apatzingen in summer at sunrise,

I'm shadow on the beach…

—JTM

I'm a gold square fighting,

I'm the bark of a dog,

I'm "Cat Daddy" played on the radio,

I'm a blue Camaro racing down the highway,

I'm a desk covered with books,

I'm a strawberry covered with cream,

I'm a beautiful waterfall,

I'm an apple tree standing in my yard,

I'm a shiny sax played by men,

I'm a snake slithering in the street,

I'm a red fire slinking in a stove,

I'm Tumbiscatin in summer,

I'm a naughty shadow…

—JM

*ELD: English Language Development

These poems were written by Newcomers to the United States using a student and teacher-generated word bank and a template, or series of prompts, created by poet and author Susan Goldsmith Wooldridge (1996, *Poemcrazy: Freeing your life with words*).

New from ReVision Publishing

THE LIGHT IN THE DARK: THE SEARCH FOR VISIONS

Ruth-Inge Heinze
Foreword by Stanley Krippner

Only $19.95
Includes shipping

264 pages

Order from:
ReVision Publishing • PO Box 1855 • Sebastopol, CA 95473

Writing the "Stories" to Right the World

Jan Ögren

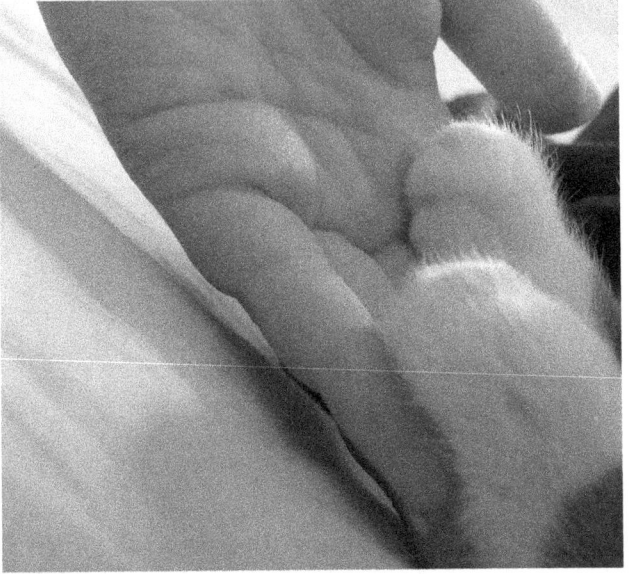

Photo by Kaplan

Story-telling is not just for bedtimes. We tell ourselves stories constantly. We are the main characters in the drama we create, which we call our lives. Often we think that who we are is already established or beyond our control, but with a few simple edits we can become different people.

When I refer to the stories we tell ourselves, I'm talking about the inner dialogue that often gets mistaken for "truth." We might discount it as just thinking. But if you start listening to the voices in your head you'll notice you're creating stories: "I need to feed the cats, put out the recycling, and remember to grab my briefcase before going to work." It might not sound like an interesting story, but it's a story as much as: "Once upon a time a girl in a red cape fed the cats, put the food scraps in the garden and picked up her basket to head to grandmother's house."

Jan Ögren, MA, MFT is a licensed psychotherapist, an international author and a storyteller. She works with clients to help them create loving stories to facilitate health and good relationships. Her love of storytelling came from her mother and her thirty plus year apprenticeship with Native American Healers. She presents at numerous conferences and workshops. You can view videos of her presentations and more of her writing, including *Dragon Magic: Amazing Fables for all Ages*, and at www.JanOgren.net.

Most of us are good in creating future fantasy stories like: "I'm going to be late and the boss is going to be mad. I'll lose my job!" Our stories have dialogue too as we imagine other's comments. "When Jasper said, 'You can't ask for that. Who do you think you are?' I should have said, 'I'm me and I'm worth it.' Why did I just hang my head and take it again?" Often, not only do we write our own scripts, we write other people's responses to us. For example: "I really need to settle this with Chris. But if I say, 'I need to talk to you,' Chris will walk away. Maybe I should try this evening. I'll start with, 'How was your day?' Chris will say, 'Busy as usual.' Then I can respond, 'Why don't you tell me about it.' Then I can casually slide into what I really need to say."

As I type on the computer, I'm creating a story in my head about how writing this article will encourage people to pay attention to their inner voices so that they can create more freedom in their lives and for those around them. This narrative helps me to actually spend the time crafting the article and enjoy doing it. If the tale I was telling myself went something like: "Everyone will think my article is not intellectual enough. They won't like the story and they'll think the exercises are dumb and won't do them." Those thoughts would depress my energy, leach away my creativity, ruin my joy in writing and may cause me to miss the deadline.

Do any of these inner-dialogues sound familiar? PAUSE. Listen to the story in your head right now. Who are the main characters, beside yourself? If a tiny fairy crawled up your shoulder, curled up by your ear, and listened to your personal thoughts, what would it hear? What impression would it get of the main character? Is s/he adventurous? Stupid? Brilliant? Fun? Boring? Is s/he likely to succeed or fail? If the fairy whispered something in your ear, what would you expect it to say? What would you like it to say?

Right now, listen to yourself. If you

can actually write your responses down it will help clarify what your personal narrative is. You can use a journal if you have one, or make notes for yourself on your phone or computer. Write what your story is now. What is the setting, and the motivation for the characters? (That is, where are you as you read this article? Why are you reading it? And what are you hoping to get from it?) Once you have answered these questions, then you can explore: how does the story you're creating affect you? Does it make you feel good? Does it make it hard to get through the day? How will it affect your willingness to explore the suggestions and be open to the story you read here? Finally ask yourself: "Is there anything I want to change about this story?

Not only do we create narratives about ourselves, we are skilled at writing scripts for others. There was a classic experiment in education referred to as the Pygmalion Effect. The experimenters randomly chose certain students in each class. At the beginning of the school year the teachers were then told a story about these children. They were the smart ones. They'll be easy to teach. You should expect them to really advance this year. The stories weren't based on anything related to the individual child. Yet at the end of the school year, each child in the randomly preselected group was performing significantly better than the other students.

This demonstrated the power of writing a story about someone, before you even meet him or her. Not only are we affected by our own inner dialogues, we also affect others by what we tell ourselves about them. That effect can be long-lasting, as people have a tendency to continue the tales in their mind, even when they are no longer around the person who first told it to them. This is especially true of children, who are learning to create their personal narratives, often with a pressure to publish them too soon. Children hear things like: "He loves to build with his blocks. He's going to grow up to be an architect/carpenter/engineer." "She's so graceful, she'll become a ballerina." Switch the gender in the prior two sentences and you can get a sense of how strong the gender stories are: "She loves to build with her blocks. She's going to grow up to be an architect/carpenter/engineer." "He's so graceful, he'll become a ballerina." Children often internalize the stories they are told growing up: "I'm good at_____." "I can't do_____." "A good girl/boy likes to_____." These messages can influence our choices in life without our even being aware of their power.

> I have discovered through working with people for more than thirty years that having a cognitive grasp of a concept is only the first step in changing it.

For a demonstration of the incredible variations in stories people can tell themselves I recommend the movie *Happy*. It's a documentary about what makes people happy. It starts by finding joy in the slums of Kolkata, India. Then it goes around the world exploring the happiest and the most stress-filled countries. After watching it I recommend reading about how this movie changed the director's life. It's the story of how he sold his house in San Francisco and moved into a trailer near the beach and started a family.

I have discovered through working with people for more than thirty years that having a cognitive grasp of a concept is only the first step in changing it. Even if you think you have a good understanding of how criticism affects you and others, I invite you to see it, feel it in your body and experience it in relationships. Hopefully that will expand the avenues available for you to edit the story of your life into the healthiest, happiest one possible. I'm going to offer some exercises to help increase your awareness, and invite you to go beyond the mental into the physical, visual and emotional.

EXERCISE ONE: The Effects of Self-Judgments on Performance.

This exercise is best done alone in a quiet place. So if you are reading this article on the bus or in a public place you might want to skip the exercises and come back to them later. You can go ahead a few pages to "The Butterfly Girl" and read that story first if you wish.

For best results, so that your rational mind doesn't write a story about the exercise before you even have a chance to experience it, try to avoid reading the full directions until you have time to actually experience it in its entirety. Do them in sequence and finish part one before reading and doing part two and three.

You will need three sheets of plain, unlined paper, a collection of colored pens, pencils or crayons. Give yourself about 10-15 minutes for it. If you keep a journal, you might want to have it available so that you can write about your experience.

PART ONE:

Stare at the empty piece of paper. Tell yourself how bad you are at drawing. And even if you can draw some things you can't do it as well as others. You especially can't draw a tree. They never look like they're supposed to. Add in anything critical that fits for you. Take a minute to do this. Then check how is your stomach feeling? What about your breathing? How do your hands feel? How much are you looking forward to drawing a tree? What emotions are you aware of? Make some notes on the top or bottom of the page in answer to these questions. Now draw a tree. And don't make any mistakes!

When you're done, check in with yourself: how are you feeling? What do you notice in your stomach, your hands, your breathing? What emotions do you feel looking at the tree? How long did you spend drawing it? Do you want to do it again? Make a few more notes, then turn the page over so you can't see it.

PART TWO: BREATHE.

Stand up. Shake your arms and hands around. Smile, even if you don't feel like it. Your body recognizes the signals from mouth-curved-upward and automatically opens the endorphin channels so you feel better. Make the smile broader. Scrunch your face up and try to wiggle your nose. Now sit back down and grab a crayon, pencil or marker and on a new sheet of paper scribble. Move your hand around so that you can feel it in your whole arm and shoulder. Scribble like you are two or three years old. If you want to create images, that's fine, the sillier looking the better. While you are scribbling tell yourself how fun this is. It doesn't matter what it looks like because you're having fun. Now throw in how good you are at drawing things, especially trees. If it helps to wipe out any messages you may have received growing up imagine the person who said something and draw a silly stick figure of them then stick your tongue out at them.

PART THREE:

Take the last piece of paper and make notes on how you are feeling. How does your stomach feel? What about your breathing? What do you notice about your hands, your shoulders? How much are you looking forward to drawing a tree? What emotions are you aware of? After you've made a few notes at the top or bottom of the page. Take a few more breaths, smile and draw a tree. Have fun!

When you're done, check in with yourself: how are you feeling? What do you notice in your chest, your hands, your breathing? What emotions do you feel looking at the tree? How long did you spend drawing it? Do you want to do it again? Make a few more notes.

Now look at the two trees. What do you notice? How much detail was in each of them? Which one do you enjoy looking at more? If there is a real visible difference between them store those pictures in your mind. Instead of just thinking of the critical voice in your head you now have a picture related to it. You also have one that you can visualize anytime you want to switch your thoughts from discouraging to enjoying. You can name the trees to make it easier to use them to help remember how you felt each time.

VARIATION:

This exercise can also be used with groups or in a classroom. Make sure and start with the critical part so that you end with the positive feelings. People can share their drawings and what they experienced. Hearing others talk about their inner-dialogues, both self-criticisms and positive judgments can normalize our own experience. Too often we are stuck in our own minds not knowing that others are experiencing similar inner-stories. Because of shame and embarrassment, we don't share and learn that we are actually "normal."

If you did read exercise one before doing it (which is very normal), what was the story you told yourself about it? How does it match or not match the actual experience? Were you telling yourself some version of: "I already know the results, so there's no point in doing it." How does that story affect your life and your ability to change your script? Often our society gives messages regarding how we should be efficient: don't take the time to FEEL you should already KNOW.

EXERCISE TWO – The Effects of Judgments on Others.

PART ONE:

This is a more subtle version of exercise one. You will need someone to do this exercise with: either a child or an adult. Get paper and crayons or something to draw with. Use the same thing both times so your rational mind doesn't tell you the story that any difference is due to the tool used for drawing.

Then ask someone to help you with a project you are doing. Tell them you need to collect a variety of hand drawn clocks--two from each person.

Start with the negative. Don't say anything out loud. Just hand them the paper and ask them to draw a clock. In your mind tell yourself the story that they can't draw. They'll mess it up. Keep your mind full of negative, critical thoughts about their ability to create an accurate clock.

After they draw the first clock put that one away. Now change your mind. Don't SAY anything to them about how well they can draw. Just imagine to yourself that they are going to create the most unique, beautiful, amazing clock and you are looking forward to seeing it.

Now hand them the paper and ask them to draw a clock again. As they are drawing, feel as much love and enjoyment as you can for them and their artistic ability.

You can also time how long they took to draw each clock and check with yourself how you felt about the time. Did it feel longer or shorter when you were feeling negative?

Feel free to talk with the person afterwards. You can ask them what their experience was with clock one and clock two. Repeat PART ONE with someone else. Trying this with several people will give you a different experience each time.

PART TWO:

Remember – it works best if you DO the exercise before reading further.

Look at the different clocks. Can you see a difference? Did any of the people you did it with notice a difference? If there was an effect, how does that feel?

There may have been no effect on the person. So now it's important to focus on yourself. How did you feel doing it? What was happening in your body? How did your stomach/shoulders/hands feel when you were being critical? How did your body feel when you were feeling supportive and loving? How long did the length of each time feel? Were you more impatient during one than the other? Which was easier to do? How did you create the thoughts for the one that was harder to sustain? What were your expectations? What was it like trying to create a certain energy field around you?

> Smile, even if you don't feel like it. Your body recognizes the signals from mouth-curved-upward and automatically opens the endorphin channels so you feel better.

VARIATIONS:

You can also try this with animals; dogs especially are susceptible to our energy fields. Pick some activity like walking your dog, playing fetch or whatever you usually do. First feel angry and critical, then very joyful doing it. See if you notice a behavior change with the dog. How did it feel for you to do it? When I tried this with my Labrador, he began to howl as I was feeling negative and danced around as I switched to positive.

You can also try doing a project with someone or asking someone to help you. Something like cooking, sorting or cleaning up. Start with thoughts of how messy and awful they are. They never do anything right. Now change thoughts and make them about how much fun you are feeling doing this project with them. Focus on how great they are to be around and how it's a big help just to have someone to cook/sort/clean up with.

If you try this with several people you can see the differences. Some people will pick up on your energy and for others it will have no effect at all. But YOU are the one most affected by your thoughts. How did your relationship with each person change as your thoughts changed?

EXERCISE THREE: Taking a Tour of Your Mind.

This exercise is designed to be done after exercise one and two.

Now that you've been practicing changing your thoughts, let's explore HOW you were able to do it? We often live with the myth that "I can't change my thoughts. It's what's true. I really am ……" But we can change our thoughts. We insert new pieces of information all the time. A friend tells us she is going to be gone all summer visiting family. We adjust, thinking we won't see her for a while. Then she says her family decided to visit here. We change our expectations to not only will we be seeing her, but getting to meet her family too.

During the exercises you changed the basic feel and flavor of your thoughts. You didn't have to do it perfectly to have experienced it. (Another common myth is: "If I can't do it perfectly it doesn't count.) You might have felt silly being negative or had critical thoughts jump in while trying to be positive. The more you practice, the more skilled you can become in changing your view of yourself and others.

Often people don't want to think negative/critical thoughts for fear they will get stuck in them, or because they do feel yucky (technical term for upset stomach, cramped shoulders and depressed energy) already. Imagine that each different way of thinking is like a room in your house with hallways in between. As you were switching from one type of thought to another it was like getting up and moving between the rooms.

> We often live with the myth that "I can't change my thoughts. It's what's true." But we can change our thoughts.

Photo by Kaplan

First you had to realize there were other rooms, then find the door, then open it and walk out. Then you turned to go to a different room. Maybe you opened a door and realized you were back in the same room. So you closed it and went looking again until you found the new room, opened that door, went in and closed it behind you.

These exercises literally encourage you to take a tour of your mind. You practice going from one room to the next. You can now use that knowledge, especially if you find yourself lost in the self-critical room. Remember that it's just one room and a choice, not "the truth." Look for the door. Pretend you are doing the exercise again. Smile, breathe, do whatever you did before to change your thoughts. Walk through your "house" and decorate each room so that you can easily identify it. You can put signs on the walls. What kind of furniture would be in each room? Practice walking between the self-critical, and the self-loving rooms, until you know the way, and can easily change your mental world.

For more information on changing your thoughts I recommend the books *Buddha's Brain* and *Hardwiring Happiness* by Rich Hanson. To explore the critic in a way that doesn't lead to fighting with it (critics love arguing) try *Taming Your Gremlins* by Rick Carson.

STORY:

If you just skipped the prior section this is where you want to be and you can go back later to try the exercise on the prior pages.

The questions I just asked, related to the exercises, accessed multiple ways of knowing. We focused on thinking and intellectual understanding. We observed others and checked in with ourselves. We physically did something that we could see. We were aware of our bodily sensations. Then we took a magical tour through our mind to explore new possibilities. These different ways of learning and exploring are brought out in the story of "The Butterfly Girl."

Reading stories is a powerful way of learning, one that both children and adults relate to. Whenever I do a presentation, I try to bring in a story because there is a magical incantation that we automatically respond to. When we hear the phrase: "Once upon a time" our bodies tend to relax. Our minds open, and we tend to store the messages at a deeper level so that we can access them whenever we need help changing our view of the world.

The Butterfly Girl

(First published as: "The Little Girl Who Wanted to Know What It Is Like to Be a Butterfly")

There once was a little girl named Ella who loved to visit her grandparents in the country. They had a cozy house with a garden in back surrounded by woods. Ella loved to spend her afternoons looking at the plants and watching the creatures of the garden. Her grandpa often sat with her, telling her the names of the birds, what they ate and what flowers and trees they liked. He taught her how to water the plants, how to pinch back the old flowers to keep the plants blooming and the best way to pick vegetables. When Ella found an odd looking bug, her grandpa always knew what it was called and what its job was in the garden.

Ella liked the flowers, the birds, and all the good things to eat. But, best of all, she loved the butterflies. They flew through the garden on the most delicate of wings, which allowed them to walk along the edge of a flower petal without squishing it. Then they'd slip their long tongues into the center of each fragrant blossom to drink its sweetness.

One day, as they were sitting next to the camellia bush watching a brown striped caterpillar chew on a leaf, Ella asked, "Grandpa, what's it like to be a butterfly?"

"That's a good question," her grandpa replied. "Let me get my books and I'll show you." He went inside and brought out four thick books filled with drawings and photographs. Together they searched for all the pictures of caterpillars, cocoons and butterflies. After he'd read her everything he had about butterflies, Ella sat next to him twirling a tiny stick between her fingers, thinking very hard. Finally she said, "I liked learning all those neat facts and the pictures were really nice, but Grandpa, I want to know what it's like to be a butterfly?"

"What's it like? Well, umm, hummm," he said, crinkling his nose and squinting his eyes as if he was trying to see an answer in the ground in front of him. "I know a way to find out!" he exclaimed, standing up quickly. Ella jumped up, ready to follow her grandpa, because he could find the answer for any question.

Around the side of the house they went past the woodpile and into the old storage shed. "Let's see what we can find in here," said Grandpa. After moving a lot of boxes, disturbing three lizards, and many spiders, he let out a cheer. "Here it is. I knew we still had it somewhere."

"What is it, Grandpa?" asked Ella, looking at a very dirty and cracked old fish tank.

"This is going to be the future home of butterflies!" he said, dusting off the tank. "Grab that old mesh screen behind you."

Ella looked around and saw the bent screen her grandpa had taken off the kitchen window last year. "This one?"

"Yep, that'll be perfect." He tore all the metal frames off until just the mesh was left. Then they took the tank, the mesh and some string and went out into the garden. First they filled the bottom with dirt, then they added twigs and leaves. "Now we go caterpillar hunting," Grandpa told Ella. They found lots of yellow and green ones, two with black spots and a very hairy orange one. Grandpa helped Ella place them on the sticks. Then he put the wire mesh over the top and secured it with the string so the caterpillars couldn't climb out. When they were finished, they put it in a corner of the back porch. "All you have to do is keep it filled with tasty leaves, watch it closely and soon you'll learn what it's like to be a butterfly." Grandpa explained

Ella checked it every day, while the caterpillars ate and ate and ate. After a few weeks, one by one, they all built cocoons. Then it was really boring because nothing happened for a long time. Grandpa decided to cut one of them open to show Ella what was inside. At first she was very curious, but all they found were strange parts of a half way caterpillar, part way butterfly and lots of yucky mushy stuff. Then she was very sad because that caterpillar would never get to learn what it was like to be a butterfly. She thought that was Grandpa's worst idea ever.

One day when the flowers had been blooming for many weeks, Ella was passing by the back porch when she noticed movement in the old fish tank. A cocoon was shaking and quivering. "Grandpa, Grandpa! Come see what the caterpillars are doing," Ella yelled as she raced back into the house.

"Those aren't caterpillars anymore," Grandpa said, as he joined her on the porch. Then he took the top off the tank and carried it to the garden. Ella and her grandpa watched as one of the cocoons opened and a beautiful orange butterfly emerged. It clung delicately to its old home, opening and closing its wings in the sun. With a little spring it launched itself into the air, followed by Ella who ran behind. She jumped in circles on the ground as the butterfly flew back and forth among the flowers and trees. Over the next three days many different butterflies emerged, striped and dotted in browns, oranges, reds and yellows. They were dressed in all the colors of the flowers and the earth. After the last one had come out of its cocoon and Ella had danced around the yard with it, she walked slowly over to her grandpa. "Grandpa, that was fun watching them come out of the cocoons. But I still don't know what it's like to be a butterfly"

Her grandpa drummed his fingers against his chin as he thought very hard. "I'm sorry Ella, I don't know any other ways to explain to you about butterflies. We've gone through all my books and you got to see how they're born. I don't know what else there is to teach you."

Ella walked away and sat down by the woods to stare at the butterflies dancing with the flowers. The summer continued with birds to watch and vegetables to eat. Sometimes Ella saw a butterfly she was sure she had witnessed being born. It would fly around the garden enjoying the daisies and daffodils.

Fall came, school started and she spent less time in her grandparents' garden. Then one Saturday, near the end of October, her grandparents took her into town to get a costume for Halloween. As they walked down the sidewalk trying to decide which store to go into first, they passed a secondhand store they had never noticed before. In the center of the display window was a shimmering butterfly costume. The body and wings were all shades of yellow and orange, and it had black tights to go with it.

"That's my costume! I want that one." Ella shouted, bouncing up and down in front of the store. It was exactly her size, so they bought it for her. As soon as they got home, Ella pulled the costume over her head and slipped her legs into the tights. There were fluffy pink antennae sticking out of a barrette that she fastened onto her head. Then her grandmother helped her slip the wings over her shoulders and attach them to her back. After Ella put it on, she ran around the garden, jumping and hopping and smelling flowers. Her grandparents got so tired from watching her that they had to sit down. As her circles around the yard grew smaller and smaller her Grandpa called out to her, "Hey, there's the prettiest butterfly I've seen all year. Now do you know what it's like to be a butterfly?"

Ella stared out into the woods beyond the garden for a few moments. She wanted to agree and say: yes, I know just what it's like to be a butterfly. She almost said it, but instead she looked her grandpa straight in the eye and said, "Grandpa, I know a lot about what it's like to be a girl running about in a butterfly costume, but no, I don't know what it's like to really be a butterfly."

They all stood there for a moment and then her grandma smiled at her and went inside. There was something about the way her grandma smiled that made Ella run after her calling "Grandma, Grandma! Do you know how I could find out what it's like to be a butterfly?" Her grandma sat down at the kitchen table and looked at a picture of her own grandmother that was hanging on the wall. It was a faded brown photo of a tall, old woman standing next to a tree with a deer sniffing her outstretched hand. Ella glanced at it, then back at her grandma. "You do! You do!" She sang as she danced around the table. "You know how I can find out what it's like to be a butterfly."

"Yes, I do," Grandma agreed. "But it's not going to be easy. What you are asking for is to see and feel the world as if you were something else. It's hard enough understanding how other people see the world, let alone a flying butterfly! It's not something you can read about or observe or pretend...."

"I know, Grandma. I tried all those other ways. It did teach me some things and some of it was really fun. But it didn't teach me what I really want to know."

Grandma paused until Ella was quiet and listening again. "It will take time and a lot of patience, so I want you to think about it. If you decide you really, truly in your heart, want to know, then I do know a way you can learn it. But you'll have to do exactly what I say. And even then you won't know until spring."

"Oh yes, Grandma, I want to know. I'll do everything you say. If I do a good job can you show me by Thanksgiving?"

Grandma just smiled at her and said, "It's not about showing you. It's helping you to learn in a different way. I want you to think about it for three days first. Then, if you still want to know what it's like to be a butterfly, I'll help you."

She stood up and started to prepare dinner, as Ella pleaded, "But Grandma, I already know. I've known all summer. Please, please, can't I start now?"

Grandma handed her a bowl full of peas in the pods. "Shell these and we'll have them tonight with some basil and thyme from the garden." Ella chewed on her lower lip and tried not to say anything else about butterflies while she helped her grandma with dinner.

Three days later she ran over after school and told her grandma, "Yes. I want to know what it's like to be a butterfly. I'll do whatever you tell me."

"Okay, we'll do it in the spring. That's when it's butterfly time," her grandma told her.

Ella thought the winter was the longest one ever. Every time she tried to get her grandmother to talk about butterflies, she'd look outside and say, "It isn't that time of year yet, just think about caterpillars for now."

When the weather finally warmed up, Ella announced to her Grandma, "I saw a caterpillar today. Can you teach me how to be a butterfly now?"

"Well," her grandma replied, "that's a sure sign of spring coming if I ever heard one. If you're going to learn to be a butterfly, you'd better do what the caterpillars are doing now."

"They're eating all the new leaves off the azalea bush you love so much."

"Little girls don't need to eat that kinda stuff, but you've got the right idea. It's time to eat and drink a lot," Grandma said. Then she quickly walked outside to see if she could convince the caterpillars to eat another plant instead of her favorite flowering bush. For the next few weeks Ella ate and drank everything her grandma gave her. She also watched caterpillars, just in case there was anything else they were doing that was important, but all they seemed to do was eat.

One Saturday morning, two weeks later, when Ella sat down at the breakfast table, she noticed there was nothing there: no juice, no fruit, no cereal or toast, not even a muffin. Her grandma patted her gently on the shoulder, while saying, "Go up to your room and put on your most comfortable clothes. Bring a warm sweater too." When Ella came down, they went out to the garden together. Near the woods was an assortment of cardboard, blankets and the plastic sheets her grandpa used to cover the vegetables when it got too cold at night. Grandma sat her down and explained how she could use all these things to build a nest big enough to crawl into. She finished by saying, "To know what it's like to be a butterfly you'll have to build a cocoon for yourself and stay in it until you know. Do you still want to do it?"

"You mean I'll have no food or water? And I can't get out and play at all?"

"Yes."

"But Grandma, it took weeks and weeks for the caterpillars to change!" Ella said, remembering how she had watched them last year.

"Well, for little girls it usually takes one day and one night. I won't think badly of you if you decide not to do it. I'll still love you and be proud of you just the same. It's your choice."

Ella bit her lower lip and tried to quiet the uneasiness stirring in her stomach. "I want to do it."

So Ella, with the help of her grandma, built herself a cocoon. The blankets made a soft, warm nest with the cardboard forming the sides and top and over it all they draped the plastic to protect her from the dew. While they were working on it, Grandpa came by asking questions. "Shouldn't she take some water in at least? Won't she be too cold at night? What if she gets scared?" He kept talking on and on as the two of them worked. He walked away shaking his head after they crawled underneath the cardboard together to try to arrange the blankets so there would be a little room to squirm around in.

Just as the sun started to peek above the trees, they finished the cocoon. Then it was time for Ella to climb in. Her Grandma closed up the entrance, reminding her once more, "If you have to come out before one day and one

Illustration by Scott Fray. Used by permission of Ruth-Inge Heinze, (1994) editor The Bear Knife and Other American Indian Tales. *Bramble Books.*

night are finished, I won't think badly of you."

The first hour passed quickly. Then the second hour took longer. By the eighth hour Ella decided she knew exactly what a caterpillar feels like while it's waiting to be a butterfly. It was very boring, a little scary and she got very thirsty and hungry. By the time the sun was setting and it was getting colder Ella wanted to crawl out very badly, but her grandma had said that if she emerged too soon, she'd have to wait until next spring to try again. So Ella huddled in her small dim cocoon waiting for something to happen.

As it got darker and darker, the noises from the crickets and bugs got louder and louder. The birds began to sing even though it was nighttime. They all seemed to be saying, "Come out. Come out." It was coming from the top of her cocoon, not the bottom where the opening was. As Ella squirmed up to try to hear better, she noticed there was a lot of room near the top.

"Why didn't I use this space before? I wouldn't have felt so squished all those hours waiting in here," Ella said to herself as she kept crawling.

There seemed to be a light up there too. As she crept toward it, it got brighter and the sounds got louder. Soon she found herself in a circle of crickets, birds, and bugs. There was even a fluffy owl. They were all dancing around a gathering of fireflies, so bright it looked like a fire burning in the middle of their circle. When they saw Ella, they crowded around her, urging her to join them. As she danced with them, she bounced up into the air. With every jump she stayed airborne a little bit longer. Then she was floating in the sky. Looking behind her she saw huge yellow and orange things attached to her back. She was so surprised she stopped waving them and she drifted back to earth. She stood up on her six thin legs and twisted around to look over her shoulder. There were big, beautiful, butterfly wings coming out of her back, just like the costume. But now she had an extra muscle extending from her shoulder blades down the center of her back that made her wings open and close. Ella gently rose back into the air. She felt connected to everything: the other insects, the trees, the rocks; she could even taste the air and knew there would be rain the next day. Looking around she saw all the creatures and plants as her friends. Some might eat her as a butterfly and some she might eat, but not tonight, because they were all celebrating together. Ella danced in the air, fluttering around and around the circle.

In the morning she squirmed out of the cocoon she'd built for herself. She crawled out the bottom where she had come in a day ago. The top looked as small as when she and her grandmother had first made it. She slowly unbent, until she was standing tall and straight by the time her grandparents came over to her.

"Well," her grandpa asked, "do you know what it's like to be a butterfly now?"

Ella looked up at them. "Yes, grandpa, I know."

"Tell us: what's it like?"

"It's well, um, ah, um," Ella tried to say. "It's just like ... Well, you know it's kinda like ... um."

"You mean you didn't find out?" her grandpa asked. "All that work and time and you still don't know."

"I know. I know," said Ella. "I was a butterfly."

"So tell us: what was it like?" he asked again.

"Being a butterfly is just like ... well it tastes of dew ... I mean it's ... floaty ... " Ella frowned and tried again. "I'm sure it's, it's ... maybe kind o ... " She moved her arms and waved her hands at them, but the words didn't come. "I can't explain it!" Ella said, with tears in her eyes.

Her grandma knelt down beside her. "That's all right Ella. Some things just can't be said in words. After all, butterflies don't talk in words, do they?" Ella shook her head. "And you do know inside how it feels to be a butterfly, don't you?" Ella nodded. "Just because you can't explain it, doesn't mean your experience wasn't real." Ella nodded again, a grin starting to spread across her face, as she remembered the feeling of being a butterfly.

Her grandpa sat down next to them. "I understand," he said. "There are some things you learn in books, some things you understand by watching. Pretending is a good way to discover things too, but when you want to know what something feels like, it helps to learn through experience. So instead of trying to explain it with words, why don't you show us, in your own way, what it's like to be a butterfly."

"I can do that," Ella agreed, nodding her head. Her grandparents got comfortable on the ground, with their backs against a tall tree, while Ella walked a few feet away. First, she reached to the ground as though she was eating armfuls of grass and leaves. Then she hugged herself tight and knelt on the ground, covering her head with her hands. She stayed still a long time, then her grandparents heard her humming. As the sound grew louder her arms started to lift. Her head rose slowly, with her eyes tightly shut, and an expression of pure joy on her face. Her hands floated higher, pulling her whole body up. She started to twirl, dipping and fluttering her arms. She was humming loudly now and her arm/wings pulsed with the sound.

Her grandparents looked at her in awe as she circled the garden. After the third time around she came back and stood in front of them. "Can you tell now, Grandpa, that I know what it's like to be a butterfly?" Ella asked.

"Yes, I certainly can," he agreed. "You also showed me how you can't put that kind of knowing into simple words."

Grandma looked up at Ella and said, "Not only do you know what it is like to be a butterfly, you've also learned that if you want to know something, you can always find a way to explore it." Then she smiled at her granddaughter. "Even though sometimes the way you learn it is kind of strange and magical."

"Yes, that's true," said Ella, thinking of the circle of creatures she was dancing with. Then her stomach rumbled. "And I discovered something else too."

"What?" they asked her.

"When you lie in a cocoon for a day and a night without food or water, you get hungry. Can I have something to eat now?"

"Certainly," grandpa said. "In fact, we fixed your favorite breakfast to honor all the effort you put into learning what it is like to be a butterfly. Come on," he said, standing up and holding out his hands to both of them. "Let's go!" And they all walked into the kitchen together.

Using Stories for Yourself and Others:

Within the story of "The Butterfly Girl," Ella explored various ways of learning. All of them are equally valid and speak to different ways of knowing the world. Often western culture, especially in schools, will emphasize intellectual, verbal knowledge over other avenues. This story can be used to help those who learn easier by observation, imitation and exploration. It can also be helpful for those whose first language isn't English. Living in the United States they may need to rely on other ways of knowing, than just using words.

"The Butterfly Girl" also validates that knowing, without the ability to verbalize, is valid and should be respected. In the story the grandfather said. "There are some things you learn in books, some things you understand by watching. Pretending is a good way to discover things too, but when you want to know what something feels like, it helps to learn through experience."

If you have an opportunity you can share the story with children. After reading it you can explore it more. Ask them: what learning styles do you prefer? Which one is more foreign to you and harder to do? What other ways are there to gain knowledge that weren't shown in the story? What can you learn from nature that is different than the human world?

As an aide in exploring these different learning styles you can have children place their hands on their heads for book knowledge, on their legs and arms for physical knowledge, over their hearts or stomachs for internal knowing (like what Ella did when she curled inward to gain the wisdom to share her knowing with her grandparents.) Having them stretch their hands out shows learning from others. You can also create pictures for each one. For those who learn verbally, you can create words and names for each way of knowing.

So far we've explored how our thoughts affect us. Then we looked at how we can affect others: either by them picking up on our energy, or by how we change our inner world when we are around them. We took a tour of our mind to practice consciously changing our stories. Then we got to read an actual story and see how the messages about different ways of learning affect us. Now it's time for the last exercise. Let's write the story that makes our lives work best. First we have to get to know the main character.

EXERCISE FOUR: Write a Character Description.

Open up a new page on the computer where you can write and edit, or get some paper and a pencil and eraser (not a pen or marker). You can also use a journal if you have one. Write a character description for the most remarkable, amazing person you can imagine. If it helps, think of a favorite character in a movie or book. Or imagine writing this for your best friend.

You can either leave a blank space for the name or put in a name. For example: (Jose/Jane/____) is the most amazing, wonderful person. (Jose/Jane/____) is such a gift to the world. (He/She/neutral) is just amazing. (Jose/Jane/____) is creative and smart. Everything (he/she/neutral) does is just right and always enough.

Write it as if you were giving it to a child or your best friend as a special gift for when they aren't feeling good.

Now when you have it as the most supercharged, positive description you can, fill in your name in the blank places.

> Write it as if you were giving it to a child or your best friend as a special gift for when they aren't feeling good.

This is especially easy if you did it on the computer and you can use the find/replace editing option. If you wrote it out on paper, either fill in the blank or erase the other name and put yours in. Also change the pronouns so that it fits the one you prefer to use for yourself. Now reread it with your name and check how you feel.

Was it hard to insert your name? Did you avoid this exercise because you guessed where it was going? Or did you edit what you wrote thinking I might ask you to put your name in? If it was hard, try it again just to see what it feels like to read a wonderful description about yourself. What happens to your body as you read it? Do you smile reading it? Do you feel warm and fuzzy in your middle? Or are your shoulders hunched up for fear someone will see what you wrote and think you are so stuck up. Is there embarrassment lurking in your stomach?

Now take several deep breaths. Read it again, this time out loud. Pretend someone you respect wrote this about you. Breathe some more. Smile as you read it. Keep breathing deeper and smiling broader until you've read it about ten times. Put it by your bed and read it every morning and every evening until you know this character so well you can write stories about yourself and how successful you are and what a wonderful life you have.

Remember that YOU write the script for your life. The external world might give you the subjects, places and people to interact with. It will give you the challenges and surprises. But the inner-script and character description are totally under your control. You can also influence the scripts of those around you either directly or subtly. And others affect your script, so be aware of who you let edit your life. Writing the best story for yourself not only helps you. It makes the world better, because you will feel better.

References

Belic, R., Shadyac, T., Reid F., Shimizu, E. (Producers), & Belic, R. (Director). (2011). Happy [Motion Picture]. United States: Wadi Rum Production.

Hanson, R. (2013). *Hardwiring happiness*. New York, NY: Harmony Books.

Hanson, R. & Mendius, R. (2009). *Buddha's brain: The practical neuroscience of happiness, love & wisdom*. Oakland, CA: New Harbinger Publications.

Heinze, R-I. (1994). *The bear knife and other American Indian tales*. Bramble Books.

Ögren, J. (2015). "The butterfly girl" in *Dragon magic: Amazing fables for all ages*. First published as "The little girl who wanted to know what it was like to be a butterfly." Namen Press.

Rosenthal, R. & Jacobson, L. (1968). *Pygmalion in the classroom*. New York, NY: Holt, Rinehart, & Winston.

Rosenthal, R. & Jacobson, L. (1992). *Pygmalion in the classroom*. (Rev. Ed.). New York, NY: Irvington.

Ross, J. (2010, July). Roko Belic talks Happy documentary. *Paste Magazine*. Retrieved from www.pastemagazine.com/articles/2010/07/roko-belic-talks-documentary-on-happiness.html.

Poetry: Between Worlds

R.L. Boyer

Photo by Kaplan

PRECARIOUS

Precarious, the poet's stance—one foot in this world, one foot in the next. Double, the poet's vision, two-faced Janus, god of passages, gazing this way, and that: Outwardly, a numinous reality,

larger than Nature, shining through the transparent fleshiness of corporeal things—light-filled common mysteries, transfigured; inwardly, the shape of my own depths rising up from the abyss like so

many bright-colored, tropical fish—flickering, fleeting, ephemeral. There is something quite strange going on here, between the worlds: a mysterious arising, a magic mirror comprehending

itself. Along the seamless encountering of form and formlessness, along the shifting horizons of appearance and disappearance, along the mysterious borderlands where form begets

emptiness, and emptiness, form—in the eternal void of things, in the infinite shapes of nothingness—along the invisible thresholds of the double-world, between the I and not-I, the naked

image assails me from within, from without, spherical, surrounded by cosmos, infinite, eternal. A seer, a seeing, and a seen, an unfathomable, unified field of being and

becoming where, sometimes, I find myself looking at things and see them looking back at me. And with this sudden intuition, what is there left on which one can depend? So precarious,

the poet's stance—gazing inside out, and outside in, one foot in this world, one foot in the next.

R.L. Boyer is an award-winning poet, literary author, and screenwriter. Boyer is also a depth psychologist and scholar of symbolic-archetypal imagery in mythopoeic storytelling. He is currently a doctoral student in art and religion at the Graduate Theological Union and UC Berkeley.

SHASTA

Beneath the shining snowy heights of Mt. Shasta, wreathed in clouds and pale blue

sky, the wind sings nature's secrets in a torrent of whispers through a stand of

ancient pines. A raven's black call is answered in the torrid noonday sun.

Photo by Gary Newman

TRIPLE GODDESS

In the heat of the midday sun
high in the bright blue sky above

a trio of turkey buzzards circles
like the blind witches in Macbeth

performing an ancient rite, a
strange circular dance—floating in

soft spirals on invisible wind trails
over the valley exploring the

curved edges of space on feathered
wingtips within them the still-point

in everything falling.

Book Review

Attachment-Based Teaching: Creating a Tribal Classroom

by Louis Cozolino (2014) W.W. Norton & Company

Reviewed by Cristina Perea Kaplan

As a longtime middle school English Language Development (ELD) teacher, I have observed a curious phenomenon. Many students will bond to me early in the year as I empathize with their difficulties and frustrations at having to learn a new language through a scripted curriculum, and the need to adapt to a foreign culture. This bonding often creates a lovely and cohesive feeling in our classroom, especially when our numbers are low and the learning styles and personalities of the students and myself are compatible. But, by midyear or sooner, students begin to bond to one another, and often will rebel against my efforts to teach them a language that they seem to find unappealing, harsh and dry in their ears, and mouths. This rebellion, if and when it comes, still surprises, and frustrates me. But perhaps it should not.

In *Attachment-Based Teaching: Creating a Tribal Classroom,* Louis Cozolino proposes, and delivers, a challenging but surmountable route to create and maintain a classroom where "secure attachment" becomes possible and desirable for both students and teachers. This concept, drawn from the psychology of object (parent-child, therapist-client) relations was not taught in my teacher-training program. But, I believe that it is part of what effective teachers have intuitively embraced. Cozolino defines secure attachment as "the ability to be soothed by others and to experience safety through proximity. In the classroom, secure attachments to teachers and other students optimize the ability to learn" (p.10).

Cozolino's daring work did not, at first, engage me viscerally. His writing speaks its truths in a quiet unassuming prose style that lets the ideas do the prodding or, at times, pushing. This includes his grounding in brain research, which supports the Jungian and depth psychological views in my background and reaches the same conclusions—we deny our biology and that of our students at our own peril.

Perhaps his main thesis, or the underpinning for his orientation, lies in the mismatch between the focus of our modern world and the ancient roots of our brain's evolution. He says early on, "The disparity of our biological and cultural clocks has resulted in a dilemma—tribal brains navigating modern culture" (p. 29). A simple table entitled "Tribal Versus Modern Society" (p. 29) makes this split patently clear. Yet, the rest of his book lays out avenues by which to heal, or undo, very many,

if not all, of these dichotomies. While many of the ideas are not new, for example, "Democratic decision making" versus "Imposed and enforced rules" as a way of student empowerment and engagement, his roadmap, rationale, and interweaving with other tribal strands are. With them, Cozolino weaves a structure that feels supportive, encompassing, and necessary.

He proposes "Four Key Aspects of Learning," (p. 36), namely *"Safe and Trusting Relationships; Low to Moderate States of Anxiety and Arousal"* (p. 36); *"Thinking and Feeling;"* and *"The Co-construction of Narratives"* (p. 37). All of these, he supports with brain research and knowledge of the brain's evolution. He asks educators to reflect, via the "Reflection Box," how much time we spend on, or "invest in your students as people living in the world" versus "the content of your teaching" (p. 39).

He proposes nothing less radical than

standing teaching on its head: curriculum must be interwoven with "team- and relationship- building exercises" rather than the other way around (p. 39). Teacher and pupil should be placed "at the center of the educational experience" and teachers should "include a focus on self awareness, compassion, and empathy into lesson plans" (p. 39). Then he goes on to give the practical nuts and bolts directions to implement this audacious plan.

Cozolino weaves a sturdy vessel of ancient spokes and base interwoven with modern strands. Yet, this question entered my mind: Will teachers have both the self-confidence, the faith in his methods and research, the courage to take the first steps that he outlines? To, in effect, step backward in time to a tribal past, while still pursuing the agenda proposed by the educational establishment at this juncture in history? When our curriculum demands time, can we justify its demotion in favor of the humane and emotional, the connected, and empathetic? Whom do we serve--the student and his or her humanity, as well as our own, or the "industrial model" of education?

Also, one of Cozolino's prime insights—tribal classrooms should have small numbers of students—does not jibe with budget constraints experienced in many parts of this country. Large numbers of students, by necessity, divide a teacher's attention. In addition, teachers at the secondary level have at least five times the number of student contacts daily as elementary teachers—a challenge in building and maintaining meaningful connections.

But he does propose ways and means to create smallness within a large group setting. Grouping is not a new idea, but its goal here is a crucial one.

I have made personal connection a goal in my classroom, but it has become more and more difficult as my students have arrived more traumatized, or otherwise seemingly closed to connection.

Cozolino's humility, and his insight are often paired. In chapter two, for example, he says "there are countless books and websites" that give team- and "tribe- building exercises," but he goes on to say, "no book can create the tribal center of gravity established by the teacher in chief" (p. 43). He encourages the exploration of "family histories" and other means for children to become self- and culturally- aware. He also promotes the study of actual tribal cultures as a way to understand the orientation of the tribal classroom that the students, teacher, parents, and administrators co-create.

> I have made personal connection a goal in my classroom, but it has become more and more difficult as my students have arrived more traumatized, or otherwise seemingly closed to connection.

Storytelling, as I noted earlier, plays a large part in the tribal classroom. He speaks of children whose "brains, minds, and hearts have been turned off" (p. 49). Stories are a way to re-engage these students by connecting them to the characters' struggles and successes.

To create a tribal classroom may require a significant change of attitude on the part of a teacher if s/he is anything like me. For my first twelve years as a multiple-subject elementary teacher, and for the past thirteen years as a middle-school ELD teacher, I have often begun my school year with a single metaphor in my mind: that of moving an ocean-going vessel, a ship. My job was to captain this behemoth, of course, and to get it out of port and onto the open ocean. This feels like a massive undertaking every year because, for better or for worse, I have expected to travel alone without a crew, except for during my early career when an instructional aide was provided and could offer assistance.

My students, in this scenario, are passengers who have been booked passage against their will with no say on the itinerary, speed of travel, or destination! I must add that, as often as I can manage, I do remove the captain's hat and don the activity director's hat to give them choices: swimming or shuffleboard?

Now, as I think about using Cozolino's *Attachment-Based Teaching: Creating a Tribal Classroom* as a guide, a new metaphor enters my consciousness that may help me to reframe my attitude: sailboat crewmember. Unlike a ship, a sailboat would need to be sizable, but not a behemoth and would require a close-knit crew. It would also need wind. In this metaphor, sailing with the winds of reform would be relatively easy. But to sail into the wind, against the wind, would require more effort on the part of the crew. In this metaphor, the students are not passive passengers, but crewmembers who help the boat to tack into the wind—a zigzag route. As crewmembers, they would help to create a climate, a sea-code that would guarantee safe arrival of all members and equal respect for all.

In this scenario I would still remain captain, the adult in the vessel, with a desired and intended destination. But the itinerary, the speed of travel, the rotation of crew assignments could all be co-created by students. In this scenario, no one can really be passive, but must take an active role. When our route coincides with a so-called reform agenda, sailing would be easier. But if we are to transform our classrooms, we may spend some time tacking into the wind, and that will have to be a risk work taking. Among these transformations would be service-oriented projects that can be "directed toward a goal for the members of the class or a project that serves others (p. 42)."

We may undertake a "heroic journey," as Cozolino discusses (pp. 186-191). It may seem to take us off course, but will ultimately lead to a destination where we will arrive with a sense we have created our journey together, endured challenges, weathered storms, grown as fellow travelers, but arrived safely as a bonded and cohesive team, or better, a tribe.

I highly recommend that you take this journey with this essential and timely guide. I believe *Attachment-Based Teaching: Creating a Tribal Classroom* by Louis Cozzolino to be both practical, and potentially transformative for teachers, students, and therefore, to society and its future.

SHAMANS OF EURASIA

New from
ReVision Publishing

$45.00
Pre-order Now

Mihály Hoppál

ReVision Publishing • PO Box 1855 • Sebastopol, CA 95473

Subscribe to ReVision - A Journal of Consciousness & Transformation

Individual Subscriptions			
	Online Only	Print Only	Online & Print
1 Year	$36	$36	$48
International		$72	$84
2 Years	$60	$60	$79
International		$96	$115
3 Years	$72	$72	$96
International		$108	$132
Institutional Subscriptions			
1 Year		$98	$134
International	$134	$191	

For new subscriptions or for renewals by mail, send your request and a check to:

ReVision Publishing • PO Box 1855 • Sebastopol, CA 95473

For new subscriptions or for renewals online, go to:

http://www.revisionpublishing.org/subscriptions.html

www.ingramcontent.com/pod-product-compliance
Lightning Source LLC
Chambersburg PA
CBHW081637040426
42449CB00014B/3354